ROTTEN

MARC J. EPSTEIN
KIRK O. HANSON

ROTTEN

WHY CORPORATE MISCONDUCT CONTINUES AND WHAT TO DO ABOUT IT

LANARK PRESS

Published by Lanark Press, Los Altos, CA
Lanarkpress.com

Production and editorial by Girl Friday Productions
Design: Paul Barrett

Image credits: cover © Shutterstock/Freer

Library of Congress Control Number: 2020913419
ISBN (hardcover): 978-1-7353361-0-7
ISBN (paperback): 978-1-7353361-1-4
ISBN (ebook): 978-1-7353361-2-1
First edition

CONTENTS

PREFACE

Corrupt and destructive behavior by executives and businesses of all sizes is a persistent and troubling feature of modern American and global capitalism. Rotten corporate conduct holds back our economic development and sows doubt that business and the free-market system contribute to a better society. Despite decades of attempts to rein in misconduct, the problem continues to fester. There is no industry or national economy that appears to be exempt.

The damage done by corporate misconduct is significant and growing. Billions of dollars of investor money have been lost as a result of fines, lawsuits, and stock market reactions. Consumers have been mistreated and injured and have had their lives disrupted. Employees have been abused and lost their jobs; some have lost their lives. In its various forms, corporate misconduct has imposed significant costs on individuals, communities, industries, and economies—and on the corporations themselves.

Why does corporate misconduct persist? Haven't corporations implemented more and more elaborate ethics and compliance programs in recent years? Haven't CEOs repeatedly proclaimed to their organizations that integrity is a corporate value? Haven't business schools added ethics and corporate responsibility studies to their required curricula? Indeed, all these efforts have occurred, yet none seems to have made a difference.

WHY WE WROTE THIS BOOK

We have spent most of our careers working on questions of business ethics and responsibility. We have been professors at several of the most prominent business schools in the world, including Harvard, Stanford, INSEAD (European Institute of Business Administration), Rice, and Santa Clara. We have advised dozens of major companies on the design of their corporate ethics and responsibility programs and on how to handle scandals that have occurred. We have given untold numbers of speeches to students, executives, and the public.

Regretfully, we have to admit that our efforts and those of so many others in the business world have failed to reduce the plague of repeated misconduct. We have taken a hard look at what we and a host of other individuals and institutions have done to address the problem. This book is an insiders' account of what has been attempted to date—and why it has failed.

In the following pages, we examine in depth why corporations misbehave. We evaluate the thus-far-unsuccessful efforts of CEOs, boards, corporate ethics and compliance officers, business ethics professors, and a phalanx of consultants and critics. We conclude there are some things that can be done now to change the sorry record to date, but we believe that the way corporations and society view ethics, compliance, training, and responsibility must change dramatically.

Too often, we hear that greed and misconduct are simply unchangeable features of capitalism. We hear that people, organizations, and the system are all corrupt. We think otherwise.

Although we believe the efforts of the past fifty years have indeed failed to stem the tide of corporate scandals, our decades of experience in working with companies, with leaders, and with students also give us some hope. We are convinced that business ethics can be improved significantly through a radical reexamination, rethinking, and redesign of the way people and organizations approach the challenges of creating and sustaining corporate integrity.

We know some have given up on reforming business. Typically, they articulate three specific explanations for the ethical failures of businesses:

1. *Some people are bad.* Many argue that the blame should be focused on the schools, families, and churches that have failed at teaching the ethics necessary to be a responsible adult. Thus, there is little that companies can do with employees who lack the required ethical foundations. In this book, we call this the *bad-apple* theory.

2. *Some companies are bad.* Others argue that it is most often not the fault of the individual employees but rather the systems of incentives, rewards, performance evaluation, governance, and control in organizations that permit and sometimes even encourage unethical behavior. We call this the *bad-barrel* theory.

3. *The economic system itself is bad.* Still others suggest that particular industries, geographies, or marketplaces are so corrupted that it is difficult for ethical individuals or organizations to survive unless they

adopt the corruption around them. We call this the *bad-orchard* theory.

We agree that there are indeed "bad apples," "bad barrels," and "bad orchards" in virtually every business sector, but we argue that there are ways to manage each and improve corporate behavior—if we are ready to take a significantly different approach to doing so.

This book, in part, was written to address the question that continues to haunt all of us who champion capitalism and the free market: Do the flaws of the market system inevitably lead to unethical and corrupt behavior in business? Is this an unsolvable problem? On this point, we are relatively optimistic. We don't believe every single corrupt action can be eliminated from business, but we do think that the increasingly troubling problem of corporate misbehavior can be reined in and that capitalism can be harnessed to serve the common good more reliably.

ARE THINGS GETTING WORSE?

While we don't argue here that corporate behavior has necessarily gotten worse in recent years, we certainly don't believe it has gotten better. Misconduct remains prominent in daily headlines, even as other crises plague our world. Companies in our most respected industries—aircraft manufacturers, banks, pharmaceutical developers—repeatedly demonstrate a willful disregard for the interests of employees, customers, business partners, the public, and even shareholders. Consider just a few of the best-known scandals:

- In 2008, widespread financial manipulation and outright fraud by respected banks and mortgage companies brought the economy to its knees. Hundreds of thousands lost their homes and jobs.

- In 2014, General Motors issued a massive recall relating to ignition switches on approximately eight hundred thousand vehicles. In order to avoid expensive required testing, an employee had given a new part the same number as an old part. When it was installed, the new part often failed, leading to over one hundred deaths in unnecessary accidents.

- In 2015, the #MeToo movement on social media caught fire, leading to the public disclosure of some of the worst instances of sexual harassment and exploitation of women in business and finally motivating companies to take action. The Black Lives Matter movement, which began in 2013, expanded this intense scrutiny to corporate opportunities for all people of color.

An argument for moral decay and failure in business could be built on these cases alone. Most of this kind of behavior occurred in companies that have extensive and long-established "ethics programs," anchored by ethics codes that explicitly state the company's commitment to following the law and serving the interests of its stakeholders.

Adopting a longer perspective, one would have to recognize that there has been progress in some areas, however. Corporations are no longer harboring the industrial sweatshops of the nineteenth century (at least in the developed world). The "impure" foods and drugs of the early twentieth century and the *overt* racism and exclusion practiced against minorities and women into the 1960s have substantially ended.

But a steady drumbeat of scandals, many doing damage far
beyond anything seen before, continues.

WHY IT MATTERS

Continuing corporate misconduct is a concern for every one of us,
consumers and employees alike. Can we really trust working for or
doing business with a company that has a history of misconduct?
Should we invest our retirement funds in its stock? A company
that has an ethical meltdown penalizes its investors through a
short- or long-term decline in share value. It may be fined millions
and now even billions of dollars. When a crisis occurs, will we be
left out in the cold?

Because corporations are such a major facet of our society, it
is important to know why misconduct continues and what can
be done about it. Most corporate executives and rank-and-file
employees would rather work for a company with genuine integrity than one whose reputation has been marred. Ethics and compliance officers would like to understand why their programs fall
so short and what they must do to make them effective. Business
school professors, particularly those who teach ethics, would like
to know why their courses don't always influence the real-world
decisions of their students. Legislators and regulators would like
to know why law enforcement has such a small impact on corrupt
behavior and what policies might make more of a difference.

In this book, we conclude that there is significant evidence
that American business is in the midst of a moral impasse, if not a
decline. But more importantly, we provide answers to the following
questions: Where do we go from here? How do we stop the moral
decay and set American businesses on a better path toward serving
consumers, their own employees, investors, and our communities?

Companies spend millions on ethics and compliance training every year. What should they do now if they really want to inoculate their companies against unethical behavior? What can business schools do to influence the behavior of their graduates? What can legislators and regulators do to nudge or force companies to treat their stakeholders honestly and fairly?

We invite the reader to examine these questions with us, and we hope that this book ignites a renewed scrutiny of how corporate behavior can be made to serve society more reliably.

CHAPTER 1

The Persistence of Corporate Misconduct

After decades of earnest speeches by prominent business leaders, the creation of elaborate ethics and compliance programs, and beefed-up regulations and enforcement, the ethics of business have failed to improve. During this same period, leading business schools and business professors, such as the authors of this book, have introduced and taught ethics courses to at least two generations of MBA students and other business graduates. Yet rotten corporate behavior continues—and may even be increasing.

Despite an aggressive press, social media ready to condemn any misconduct, new ways of monitoring corporate behavior, and an army of ethics and compliance officers, corporate misconduct seems to continue without pause. No company seems immune; every year, yet more distinguished companies are caught engaging in serious misconduct.

In just the past fifteen years, the litany of misconduct includes massive misrepresentation by banks of mortgage-backed securities, the corrupt rating of those securities by supposedly independent rating agencies, pharmaceutical pricing that defies belief and any justification, blatant deception within two global and respected automobile companies, and financial fraud in a growing gang of enterprises. Gross misconduct is not limited to companies in the shadows of the economy but also happens in companies that enjoyed, until the moment their ethical failings were revealed, sterling reputations.

Consider the case of Volkswagen (VW), the well-respected German automaker, rightly hailed for its engineering prowess and lauded for throwing off the taint of the Nazi era to win a global reputation for responsible behavior.

The Volkswagen Emissions Scandal

We are not shocked easily, but this story did it. In 2006, a top technology executive at VW prepared a PowerPoint presentation that provided the details on how the company could cheat on the US emissions tests. A PowerPoint presentation on how to cheat!

Over the next decade, VW engineers installed software in more than eleven million cars worldwide (including VW, Audi, and Porsche models) that allowed them to fool the regulators into thinking that their cars were in compliance with air-quality regulations when indeed they were not. These "defeat devices" were able to detect when they were being tested and needed to be in compliance with emission standards. At those moments, the devices activated the pollution controls;

in normal driving mode, however, they routinely exceeded acceptable levels of emissions.

The VW scandal shocks us for so many reasons. Although the use of the devices had been ongoing for many years, it was not until 2015 that VW finally admitted that it had been selling high-polluting cars and had deliberately installed the software. One VW board member explicitly stated that because VW engines could not meet US requirements, the company developed the software to cheat the system.

The fact that it appears to have been intentional, with so many managers involved, is perhaps the most shocking aspect of this scandal. Financial costs are still being incurred and already total more than $30 billion in fines, legal claims, and recalls. These costs do not include damage to the brand, which is certain to affect future sales. Beyond financial costs, experts estimate that the excess pollution will lead to several hundred premature deaths in the United States and Europe, although it is impossible to identify specific victims. Many other stakeholders were harmed, including customers, dealers, the environment, and employees. There have been numerous criminal charges against, and guilty pleas and settlements from, both the company and some of its executives.

In 2007, VW executives had declared their goal of becoming the largest car company in the world and developed a culture oriented toward that goal. They were going to try to achieve that aim at all costs. In addition to the lax ethical standards and "culture of tolerance," the company admitted that the organizational shortcomings also included inadequate quality-control standards and systems. The pressure to achieve results was intense. VW did grow rapidly and moved up to the number one automaker in 2014.

In court documents filed by VW, the company reported that in 2006, when the cheating began, the technicians assessed the chances of being caught as small, and that may have been tempting to employees under pressure to find a solution to a troubling problem. Hans Dieter Pötsch, chairman of the VW supervisory board, admitted that the cheating took place in a climate of lax ethical standards. "There was a tolerance for breaking the rules," he said. "It proves not to have been a one-time error, but rather a chain of errors that were allowed to happen."

And this was not the only scandal going on at VW at the time. In 2005, it was discovered that managers and labor representatives had received improper benefits from the company and its suppliers. A quid-pro-quo agreement had developed between management and labor that centered on the important role that union representatives play on German boards (with labor having 50 percent of the seats on supervisory boards). However, not all shareholders were receiving equal benefits, and the VW board was not protecting the minority shareowners.

VW is an example of serious corporate misconduct occurring in multiple dimensions, but it is perhaps most galling that all of it was intentional. So many corporate leaders knew it was wrong and did it anyway. Many senior corporate leaders and senior engineers were involved in the fraud, but an even larger number of managers knew about the deception and failed to take any action. The CEO and several other senior executives lost their jobs, but many more were complicit.

We should not be surprised that such an event occurred at VW. The structure of the company made it crisis-prone rather than crisis-prepared. With the Piëch and Porsche families having more than half of the voting shares and in control of the board, the company exhibited few of the characteristics of good corporate governance. It was insular and had a small number of independent directors. Sometimes corporate misconduct is fraud; other times it is poor systems or poor oversight. In VW, all aspects of corporate misconduct were there—fraud, cover-up, poor governance, and intentionality.

The global reaction to the revelation of VW's duplicity was predictable. The company was condemned by anti-corporate activists, government officials, and innumerable editorial boards. The VW case, however, is not as surprising when set against the growing list of blue-chip companies that have had similar moral meltdowns.

Documenting the continuing incidents of corporate misconduct is not difficult. There are many egregious cases in the recent past we can cite from memory. Exhibit 1-1 presents just some of the major scandals that have garnered public attention over the past twenty years.

In addition to the frequency of major corporate scandals, an important measure of the problem of corporate misconduct is the scale of disruption and damage caused by the misconduct. The 2008 global financial meltdown resulted from widespread misconduct by US banking and investment institutions, which conducted irresponsible financial transactions and misrepresented investments to consumers and other businesses. The greatest environmental disaster of modern times, which occurred in 2010 when a BP well blew out in the Gulf of Mexico as a result of ill-advised cost-shaving measures, killed eleven people and fouled beaches

EXHIBIT 1-1

WIDELY KNOWN CORPORATE SCANDALS, 2001–2020

2001—**Enron**: Financial manipulation leads to the collapse of the company

2002—**WorldCom**: Financial manipulation by the CEO and executive team results in numerous convictions

2004—**Siemens of Germany**: A systemic global bribery scheme facilitated the company's growth

2008—**Wall Street financial firms**: Deceptive practices and fake financial ratings bring the economy close to collapse

2008—**Peanut Corporation of America**: Executives cover up widespread *Salmonella* poisoning

2008—**Satyam Computer Services of India**: Financial fraud inflates earnings

2009—**Bernard Madoff**: The 2008 financial crisis reveals a massive Ponzi scheme targeting wealthy investors

2010—**British Petroleum (BP) of the United Kingdom**: Deepwater Horizon oil-rig fire kills eleven and fouls the Gulf of Mexico

2010—**Massey Energy mines**: Neglect of basic safety standards leads to multiple deaths

2012—**Facebook**: User privacy is compromised; similar incidents follow

2013—**Rana Plaza of Bangladesh**: A sweatshop building collapses, killing 1,100

2014—**General Motors**: A faulty ignition switch, known about for ten years, kills 124

2014—**VW of Germany**: Illegal pollution-control "defeat devices" deceive regulators

2014—**Embraer of Brazil**: Repeated bribery to sell aircraft worldwide exposed

2015—**Takata Corporation of Japan**: Exploding airbags cause dozens of deaths

2015—**Blue Bell Creameries**: Executives ignore repeated contamination of ice cream with *Listeria*

2016—**Wells Fargo**: Telephone sales employees create millions of fake customer accounts

2016—**JPMorgan Chase in China**: Banking firm hires the sons and daughters of Chinese officials to win business

2016—**Facebook**: Failure to control Russian trolls and fake news influences elections

2017—**Equifax**: Inadequate security leads to hacker theft of millions of financial records

2018—**Theranos**: Health-care start-up sells blood tests that do not work

2019—**Boeing**: Flawed MAX pilot software leads to two airline crashes

2020—**Airbus of Europe**: Systemic global bribery to sell aircraft revealed

from Texas to Florida. The record for the most employees fired for misconduct, as well as customers betrayed, may belong to Wells Fargo, with more than five thousand sales staff fired for creating millions of fake accounts in customers' names, leading to financial havoc and hardship for many of those customers. A failure to anticipate and then confront misuse of its social media platform convinced most observers that Facebook was complicit in Russian interference in the 2016 US election.

Another measure of corporate misconduct is the size and number of fines for criminal and civil misconduct imposed on corporations. Both measures have steadily increased over the past two decades, at least until the number of fines leveled off under the Trump administration. Nonetheless, the largest US fines during the past ten years have been eye-catching: BP was fined at least $18 billion for the Gulf of Mexico oil spill; Wells Fargo, Royal Bank of Scotland, Credit Suisse, and Barclays Capital have together been fined more than $20 billion for various financial crimes; VW has so far been fined $9.7 billion for its emissions scheme; Pacific Gas and Electric has been forced to pay a minimum of $1 billion in fines and $5 billion to victims of wildfires for its neglect of safety; and in late 2019, Facebook was fined $5 billion for privacy violations. One database list of US fines for 2019 alone shows more than 1,400 corporate fines exceeding $100,000 and more than 15,000 exceeding $5,000.

The data for individual criminal punishment are much more mixed. The number of individuals convicted of white-collar business crime remains small and may even be declining. For the massive financial abuses in the 2008 mortgage meltdown—which led to a collective $44 billion in fines for the top six US financial institutions—only a single individual received jail time. This is in contrast to the conviction of twenty-four executives at Enron in the early 2000s and dozens of executives in the collapse of savings and loans in the late 1980s. Some have suggested that this trend has made executives more brazen in their misconduct.

Both critics and supporters of American capitalism and American business have sought remedies for continuing corporate malfeasance. For the harshest critics, each additional incident of fraud proves their point that capitalism is fatally flawed and needs to be reformed, if not by the public ownership of large enterprises, then by rigorous regulation and draconian punishments. For cheerleaders of capitalism, each incident makes their advocacy of economic freedom and reduced regulation harder to defend. It is indeed hard to argue for further deregulation when companies are already consistently exploiting lax regulation to engage in fraud and other deceptive practices.

A HISTORY OF REPEATED MISCONDUCT

The litany of recent corporate misdeeds just described is hardly novel. Each era of corporate history is replete with its own examples, as well as reform efforts that often follow public outrage. In the early 1900s, the power and abuses of large trusts and monopolies led to an era of antitrust enforcement. The Progressive Era of the 1920s saw the first attempts to address adulterated food and drugs. Various regulatory measures were introduced during the 1930s in the wake of the 1929 stock market collapse and the ensuing Great Depression.

The post–World War II period of the 1950s saw a dramatic economic expansion and optimism regarding civic-minded companies that contributed to their communities. This narrative was challenged by stories of disregard for automobile safety in the production of General Motors' Chevrolet Corvair and later in Ford's Pinto. Some companies finally began to address racial issues in the workplace, but only after the devastating 1965–68 urban riots. By the end of the 1960s, concern focused on the environmental impacts of the paper and energy industries. The Clean Air and Clean Water Acts, first adopted in 1970, aimed at controlling the worst of corporate environmental behavior. Only in the 1970s was any attention paid to equal opportunities for women in the workplace, although discrimination and harassment continued for decades.

In the 1970s, new attention focused on illegal corporate political contributions and, later, corporate bribery abroad. Each of these scandals ensnared dozens of blue-chip companies, putting business ethics on the national agenda. Each of these also led to significant new laws designed to rein in corporate misconduct.

The 1980s began an era of accelerated wealth accumulation among corporate elites and an increasing incentive to do whatever was necessary to grab a share of this newfound wealth. The rapid rise of fortunes on Wall Street led to numerous scandals featuring insider trading and other securities violations. An expansion of defense spending under President Ronald Reagan led to major defense contractors being exposed for deliberately overcharging on government contracts.

Rising corporate profits in many industries enabled a significant increase in corporate salaries for senior executives in the 1990s, with a surge of cases of financial manipulation and outright fraud designed to win even higher executive compensation. Shortly after 2000, a dramatic increase in financial scandals at well-regarded firms—such as Enron, WorldCom, HealthSouth, and others—led to the passage of the Sarbanes-Oxley Act of 2002. The new law increased fines, required the CEOs and CFOs to personally certify that their financial reports were accurate, and required corporate lawyers to report wrongdoing they observed in their own companies.

The financial meltdown of 2008 revealed the massive misrepresentation of mortgage-backed securities and other financial products by Wall Street firms and rating agencies. The economic collapse that followed cost investors and common citizens billions of dollars and the loss of their homes. In 2010, Congress passed the Dodd-Frank Wall Street Reform and Consumer Protection Act, which constrained the behavior of Wall Street firms and established consumer protections on financial transactions. Over the next decade, many of these new regulations would be slowly chipped away by financial industry lobbying.

FAILED EFFORTS TO CONTROL THE PROBLEM

The brief history just recounted is only a portion of the record. The series of scandals from 2010 to 2020 clearly demonstrates that Wall Street is not the only bad actor. Corporate scandals in every corner of the globe have given more evidence that this is an economy-wide and worldwide problem. Corporate misconduct and its growing impact, if not greater frequency, are threatening society.

Why does misconduct keep happening? Is it just that there is moral decay in our society, and nothing can be done about it? Is it that parents, schools, churches, and other important institutions in people's lives have failed in their role of building moral character? Should we blame the leaders and managers of corporations for the failure to establish both effective governance and ethical cultures that might limit this misconduct? Are the incentives and pressures in corporations that lead to misconduct more severe today due to an increasingly myopic focus on short-term profitability?

First, it is helpful to know what efforts have been tried—and have failed—to stop corporate misconduct. To date, society has relied on nine particular strategies to control corporate misconduct:

1. The ethics and values of individuals in business
2. Family, schools, and churches
3. Laws and regulations
4. CEO leadership and proclamations
5. Corporate ethics programs
6. Business schools and external corporate ethics training programs

7. Corporate self-regulation and voluntary industry codes
8. Corporate social activists
9. Building the "business case" that ethics is profitable

The following sections provide a more detailed discussion of each strategy.

THE ETHICS AND VALUES OF INDIVIDUALS IN BUSINESS

The first line of defense against misconduct in any area of society is the integrity of those who are making the ethical choices. Corporations have traditionally relied on the personal values of their own employees to produce good corporate behavior.

Sadly, the history of corporate misconduct consists of story upon story of individuals who did wrong. Some set out from the beginning to lie, cheat, and steal; many business scandals were simply stories of personal corruption set in a business context. Some other individuals might have acted ethically in most circumstances, but they were tempted by their own greed when there was a chance to take advantage of others or were unable to resist pressure from supervisors to engage in wrongdoing.

As we will describe in a later chapter, we have come to believe that integrity in society is distributed on something approximating a normal distribution curve. Some individuals will always do the right thing; others will always seek personal advantage even if it means doing wrong. Most of us are somewhere in the middle, desiring to be ethical but always vulnerable to temptation and pressure.

It is clear, though, that simply relying on the values and ethics of employees and executives is a losing strategy. In the wake of a major scandal, many executives proclaim, "I never thought this could happen in my company." Assuming everyone in a company will do the right thing has always been a naive assumption; today, it is nothing short of negligent.

Finally, some individuals misbehave because they are uncertain what conduct their companies and individual supervisors really want from them, and they draw the wrong conclusion. Sometimes companies and managers are deliberately ambiguous, hoping employees do whatever is necessary, even if it involves ethically questionable methods. This attitude insulates the bosses from direct culpability.

FAMILY, SCHOOLS, AND CHURCHES

Most people believe that there is a critical role in our society for families, schools, and churches to instill ethical values among both children and adults. By promoting moral lessons in homes, schools, and religious institutions, society hopes that ethical behavior will result. However, each of these institutions has failed to properly instill ethical values in the past few generations.

Critics of the modern family blame part of the perceived moral decline in the United States on weak parenting. Yet even if one's moral formation in the family is strong, it may not always promote good behaviors. Some parents believe "ripping off the system," for example, is acceptable. Others hold to absolute standards of honesty, truthfulness, and integrity.

The same concerns regarding the role of schools in shaping moral character can be made. Fifty years ago, public schools and local communities enforced standards of right behavior as interpreted by the norms of the era. Sadly, some of these norms included racism, disparate treatment of certain classes, and form over the substance of ethical behavior. When cultural standards shifted, for a time schools were hesitant to advocate for any specific value perspectives. In recent years, the character education movement, anti-bullying programs, and the social-emotional learning movement have sought to teach values of respect and compassion for all others in schools, but in part because of the opposition of some parents, most educational programs of this type have had limited effect.

Similarly, the influence and capability of religion and religious institutions to shape moral character have eroded in recent decades. The decline of church attendance and organized religion and the increasing "secularization" of American and global society have made appeals to common religious values more difficult. The moral authority of many churches has also been challenged by a succession of scandals, including sexual abuse, involving clergy and church staff members.

Religious attention to corporate behavior, however, has increased significantly over the past decades. Prior to the 1980s, religious writings focused primarily on personal virtue. Only Jewish scholars, as well as an occasional Protestant theologian, wrote extensively on the ethical obligations of businesspeople. Over the past thirty years, many more religious figures have spoken out on economic matters. Catholic popes, particularly Benedict XVI and Francis, have written about the ethical obligations of executives. Francis has emphasized corporate obligations to the environment. To date, though, such public pronouncements have had little impact on behavior.

LAWS AND REGULATIONS

Our traditional way of controlling corporate misconduct is through laws and regulations. Thousands of pages of federal, state, and local laws specify actions by businesses that are prohibited. Among prohibited actions are cheating customers, suppliers, and financial institutions; misrepresenting products and services; colluding with competitors to raise prices or divide up customers; and misusing customer data.

Most specific prohibitions are written by regulatory agencies rather than legislative bodies. Business issues are complex and demand specific guidance. Regulations focus on everything from truth in advertising, environmental guidelines, employment practices, and sanitary habits to a wide array of other business customs. Typically, regulations governing business conduct go through a deliberate process of proposal, comment, and response before they are adopted. This often gives targeted lobbying by corporations and other business interests an outsize influence on the final form of standards.

It is difficult to write and enforce standards in some areas of misconduct. It may be impossible to craft a regulation that clearly states the desired or prohibited behavior; in other cases, the cost of enforcement is too high. This leaves significant areas of corporate conduct free of regulation.

Laws and regulations, which have the force of law, require government monitoring, investigation, and enforcement. Governments have created an interlocking web of laws and regulations at the national, state, and local levels, and the task of compliance can sometimes be a significant burden for businesses. Although the point is invoked much too frequently by corporate interests, there are some regulations for which the cost of compliance is indeed prohibitive. For companies that operate in multiple states and countries, keeping up on regulatory requirements requires dozens and even hundreds of employees. The inconsistencies between laws and regulations can create a particular challenge in some cases.

The effectiveness of regulation can also change significantly given the ideology and enforcement priorities of the federal, state, or local authorities behind the regulations. For global companies, the many and occasionally conflicting laws of different countries create particular difficulties. The overlapping and conflicting regulations can themselves create ethical dilemmas regarding which laws should be followed and which can be ignored.

Most corporations and businesses seek to understand and comply with laws and regulations affecting their particular industry and business, but corporate attitudes toward law and regulation vary significantly. In many cases, businesses use their wealth and connections to persuade legislators and regulators to water down proposed regulations. Some industries are said to "capture" the regulation-writing process, giving them the ability to prevent any rules they oppose. Some companies choose not to comply with selected regulations, considering the occasional fine for noncompliance a "cost of doing business," cheaper than complying with the requirements. For others, compliance is a matter of following the letter and not the spirit of a regulation. And occasionally, some companies will simply "roll the dice," hoping they will not be caught for noncompliance.

Regulation is absolutely necessary for the prevention of corporate misbehavior, but as practiced in the United States today, it has been only partially successful. Currently, even the best-run companies are fined periodically for various aspects of their behavior. This is undoubtedly partly due to poor formulation of the laws and regulations, but it is also a result of weak and uneven enforcement.

Many corporate executives would contend, however, that with thousands of employees scattered across the country and the globe, occasional violations are unavoidable, whether due to poor judgment by the employee or misconduct by a bad apple. Thus, laws and regulations are essential to improving corporate ethical behavior, but they are insufficient to solve the problem completely.

CEO LEADERSHIP AND PROCLAMATIONS

When changes of any kind are sought in business, it is logical to ask business leaders to make it happen. Any progress on curbing corporate misconduct must begin with the support of the top business leadership nationally and the leadership in each company.

Yet corporate leaders have been very irregular in their support for business ethics and corporate social responsibility. During the 1950s and '60s, broad statements by the executives of the largest companies regarding the obligations of the corporation to society were common. The economist Milton Friedman, in a 1970 *New York Times* article, sought to reverse the trend of acknowledging such a responsibility—or at least to point out the hypocrisy of those who made such statements. He argued that "the social responsibility of business is to increase its profits" and nothing more.

Nonetheless, corporate exhortations continued, and some executives were praised for their endorsement of integrity and social responsibility. In the late 1970s, the Business Roundtable, a national association of the two hundred largest American companies, issued the first of three statements on social responsibility and ethics. It endorsed paying attention to the legitimate needs of all the stakeholders of a company. In the 1990s, the Roundtable issued a follow-up statement putting the emphasis back on serving the shareholders alone. And in 2019, the Roundtable issued yet a

third document restoring the emphasis on serving all stakeholders. The Roundtable has never explained how trade-offs between
stakeholders should be made, nor has it proposed a way of enforcing its various statements.

Since 2000, many executives have written books endorsing a
stakeholder approach to integrity and responsibility. Many of the
companies they led, however, reverted to more typical corporate
behavior when those leaders retired or moved on. Within most
companies, executive statements have rarely gone beyond general
endorsements of integrity and a broad commitment to serving
society. Such statements are often prepared by staff writers and
may or may not reflect an active commitment of the top executive.
In the wake of the collapse of Enron in 2002, copies of its ethics
code, which contained many pious, hypocritical statements from
its leaders, were sold on eBay as collectors' items.

Corporate leaders have been making speeches on corporate
ethics and responsibility to their internal corporate staff members
and to external audiences for decades, but these public exhortations have most often been greeted only as lip service.

CORPORATE ETHICS PROGRAMS

In the early 1980s, a small number of corporate leaders came to
believe they had to shore up the company commitment to values
and thus launched ethics workshops for managers. In 1983, the
late Walter Shipley, on taking the CEO job at Chemical Bank (later
merged into JPMorgan Chase), convened daylong workshops with
his senior executives to talk about their commitment to common
values. In 1985, McDonnell Douglas's CEO Sanford McDonnell
created a training program on company values and cotaught it with
a Stanford Graduate School of Business professor for all thirty-five

thousand employees. In 1986, the Defense Industry Initiative on Business Ethics and Conduct, a voluntary organization founded in response to defense industry scandals, committed the signatories to creating corporate ethics programs.

Initial efforts to institutionalize ethical behavior were feeble, consisting of the adoption of corporate codes of conduct, the promotion of annual ethics and compliance training, and the creation of the first whistleblower hotlines. Corporate institutionalization of ethics took a second leap after the 2001 adoption of the federal sentencing guidelines, directions to federal judges that authorized reductions of corporate fines and penalties if a company had instituted a good program designed to promote compliance. Companies, urged on by their general counsels, rushed to create such programs to become eligible for mitigation. Lawyers began to populate the ethics staff members of most companies, and soon the field was referred to as "ethics and compliance" rather than just "ethics." The result was that the focus shifted to adopting, often in a checklist fashion, the required structures listed in the sentencing guidelines.

As corporate ethics programs and periodic ethics training became more common in companies, efforts were made to reduce the costs of the ethics programs, which in many cases undermined the purpose and impact of the programs. The effectiveness of those programs was always unclear, regardless of how they were structured and delivered.

The implementation of ethics and compliance programs faced many obstacles. Active participation by top executives was rare, as was the visible support given to the growing cadre of ethics and compliance officers charged with implementation. Believing the programs were adopted for window dressing, middle managers frequently undermined the impact of the programs through their skepticism or outright opposition. Frequently, the actual behavior of top managers and executives so contradicted the ethics commitments that the program was dead on arrival. And because such programs were not executive priorities, they were often poorly designed and starved for funding. The typical chief ethics and compliance officer was seen as a staff officer who was not given a role or influence in major corporate decisions and issues and was considered successful if he or she did not bring major problems to senior management's attention.

One of the glaring weaknesses of most corporate ethics efforts is the attention given to it by the firm's governance system. Only recently have corporate boards felt it was their responsibility to police the ethics of the firm, and even today only some embrace that responsibility. Companies are often uncertain of how to do this or are unwilling to chastise top executives or top performers who violated the standards of a good ethical culture.

The federal sentencing guidelines were rewritten to address this failure, setting the standard that audit committees should hear regular reports regarding the implementation of the company's ethics programs, boards should hold meetings to assess the ethics and compliance risk of the firm's business and business model, and board members themselves should undergo ethics training appropriate to their functions. The Sarbanes-Oxley Act of 2002 requires boards to act decisively when accusations of misbehavior arise. Still, few companies are willing to dedicate the resources and executive time necessary to create an effective ethics and compliance program. Chapter 3 presents a more detailed critique of corporate ethics and compliance programs.

BUSINESS SCHOOLS AND EXTERNAL CORPORATE
ETHICS TRAINING PROGRAMS

Both authors of this text have been deeply involved in efforts to improve corporate behavior through business school and executive education.

In 1979, the business schools of Stanford, Harvard, and Wharton each made a commitment to introducing ethics courses. Today, business ethics is taught in almost all business schools, often as a separate required course. Many schools have additional elective courses related to individual ethics, financial or marketing ethics, corporate responsibilities, and social entrepreneurship. In addition, many schools encourage their faculty to try to integrate ethics in courses throughout the curriculum so that business ethics is not seen as a separate concept but as an important part of each of the business functions (e.g., accounting, finance, and marketing) and central to the proper and successful management of enterprises.

Most observers would conclude that while ethics courses may have done some good, many have been poorly implemented. There is frequently a lack of clarity regarding how ethics and ethical norms are to be taught, particularly in secular colleges and universities. No one is entirely sure whether education at this stage of life can change behavior or which pedagogical approach would be most effective. Many courses are empirical, or "positive" in academic jargon, describing the role of ethics in some people's decisions rather than what decisions fulfill ethical criteria. Most recently, "behavioral ethics" material has described ways in which cognitive and emotional factors lead individuals to act in ethical and unethical ways. Rarely have courses focused on normative ethics, what a businessperson or company ought to do.

At the same time that business ethics courses were being introduced, corporate finance and the primacy of the shareholder wealth model were growing in business schools. Business school students were rightly confused about the messages they were being given. And when looking to industry, or to their own companies in the case of executive students, there was scant evidence that businesses would care whether employees brought an ethics perspective to their work.

Today, most large companies include ethics and compliance topics in supervisory or executive training. However, the subjects are often addressed by a single session or speech by an outside figure, sometimes a business school faculty member. Compliance training is often limited to an annual briefing by a lawyer on current interpretations of the law. The training provided to hourly and nonmanagerial employees is most often limited to compliance with legal and bright-line rules in the company code of conduct. Ethics is rarely addressed in any depth.

CORPORATE SELF-REGULATION AND VOLUNTARY INDUSTRY CODES

In the wake of growing demands for controlling corporate behavior, some corporations have sought to head off additional regulation by establishing or embracing industry-wide codes of behavior, an exercise in self-regulation. Some of these are launched by companies themselves; others are promulgated by activists who urge companies to become "signatories" to voluntary standards.

Self-regulation has the potential to permit a more targeted design of regulatory standards. In general, regulations are written for broad categories of companies and operating situations, making compliance difficult and sometimes unnecessarily expensive. On the other hand, self-regulation efforts can lead to more lip service than genuine compliance. Usually, self-regulatory regimes are monitored and audited only by the company or other industry interests, which may lead to weaker effort or watered-down standards over time.

The typical large company participates in several self-regulatory efforts. Companies play a major role in shaping the voluntary codes, often strongly influenced by the least advanced or most resistant industry competitors. Few voluntary efforts include public auditing of behavior consistent with the initiative. Because the codes are voluntary, there are scarce mechanisms to compel compliance—or even participation in the voluntary regime. Thus, codes frequently do not encompass all major firms in a given industry.

Nonetheless, voluntary codes are widely used. Their long-term effectiveness depends on the willingness of corporate or professional leaders to write strong codes, to monitor the behavior of their competitors, and to impose whatever sanctions are part of the regime. Professional societies, including medical and legal associations, have long struggled with decisions to penalize and even remove certification from those guilty of misconduct. Such efforts seem more effective when backed up by close scrutiny by government, which has granted rights to self-regulate but remains deeply interested in controlling misconduct.

At their worst, self-regulatory regimes can actually enable bad behavior, protecting the interests of the largest firms in an industry or the longest-serving members of the professional group. They can be a cynical public relations gesture and a cover for substandard effort.

Over time, many codes constitute drags on real progress because most do not keep up with changing needs in the social, environmental, or human rights context they were meant to address. Companies often try to weaken the impact of certain codes or resist strengthening their language when they are no longer adequate. Self-regulation will always have a role in controlling misconduct, but whether self-regulation has significantly changed behavior in critical areas is debatable.

CORPORATE SOCIAL ACTIVISTS

Interest groups have long played a prominent role in pressuring corporations to act more ethically and responsibly. In the 1960s, there was a growing awareness of the issues of racism and segregation in America, consumer-product safety, and the environmental impact of corporate operations. A generation of activists, from Martin Luther King Jr. to Ralph Nader to Denis Hayes, the founder of Earth Day in 1970, grew to challenge the value consensus.

An early and successful example of corporate activism is found in the Sullivan principles. In the mid-1970s, General Motors cooperated with its activist African American board member Rev. Leon Sullivan to launch an organization that established principles for ethical corporate operations in South Africa, then a nation with rigorous apartheid laws marginalizing black and "colored" citizens. Rev. Sullivan and other activists behind the principles ratcheted up the demands of the code several times, introducing auditing and monitoring, a rating system for corporate behavior, and new requirements as the system of apartheid and the politics of South Africa evolved. The Sullivan principles are generally credited with changing corporate behavior and mobilizing corporate pressure on the South African regime, which contributed to the end of apartheid in the early 1990s.

The example set by the Sullivan principles was followed by many activists who strongly advocated for corporations to change their behavior in specific areas, such as environmental behavior, supply-chain standards, and racial progress. Some of these proposals have been effective in changing corporate behavior, but most have had little effect. In some cases, the demands were so extreme that it was almost impossible for companies to comply. In other cases, activists used tactics that drove away even those within corporations who sympathized with them.

It is also true that activists are usually resisted by companies that do not want to change their behavior or subject themselves to outsiders' influence. Only a minority of executives believe they have something to learn from the activists. Many only agree to meetings to mollify activists or because they believe such meetings will help their treatment in the press. Other executives believe that even meeting with activists gives them standing and influence. In some cases, including the environmental group Greenpeace, corporate interests and their government allies have retaliated against the activists' reform efforts through lawsuits that seek to deprive them of their resources and reduce their influence.

Activist groups are aware of this dynamic. Ceres, a long-standing environmental activist group, changed its tactics over the past twenty years to work more cooperatively with the investment community. By urging the incorporation of environmental performance ratings in investment analysis portfolios, Ceres is credited with helping change the behavior of large institutional investors. But not all activist groups have had similar success.

BUILDING THE "BUSINESS CASE" THAT ETHICS IS PROFITABLE

Efforts to promote ethical behavior in business have also included attempts to build a "business case" for corporate ethics and social responsibility. Since the 1980s, corporate executives, corporate ethics officers, and business associations have written hundreds of essays, with titles such as "The Business Case for Business Ethics" or "The Business Case for Social Responsibility," hoping to convince profit-oriented executives to take notice.

In general, the argument in these essays is that good ethics is good business and that the long-term self-interest and financial interests of shareholders are served by ethical behavior in the present. It is further argued that there is a positive financial payoff in increased shareholder value for investments in corporate ethical and socially responsible behavior.

Sometimes the "business case" is based on studies that purport to prove that the ethical or socially responsible company is more profitable, at least in the long term. Reviews of many such studies often show that the data are mixed; it is hard to make a clear case that ethics is profitable based on studies to date. Even how "ethical behavior" is defined in the study can be a point of contention. Some have used the incidence of regulatory fines to determine which firms operate ethically, but this is a very limited definition.

To date, the many attempts to conceive and present a "business case" for ethical behavior have not been effective in convincing skeptical executives or heading off misconduct. It is still too easy for companies to claim they are acting ethically or to pay more attention to reputation than actual behavior.

THE THREE WAYS MISCONDUCT HAPPENS

Learning from the failures of past efforts to control misconduct is critical to the solutions we recommend in this book, as is understanding in greater depth why misconduct happens. Corporate misconduct is not simply due to a moral collapse. It is not the fault of just bad people, bad organizations, or a corrupt economic system. It is in part due to each of these, but it is more complicated than that.

In the next three chapters, we explore in greater depth the challenges faced in trying to make progress against corporate misconduct. We believe misconduct originates in three primary areas: individual values and behavior; corporations where cultures are ethically weak and perverse incentives are strong; and competitive environments that make it difficult, if not impossible, for corporations and their employees to do the right thing.

ARE INDIVIDUALS TO BLAME? THE BAD-APPLE THEORY

The explanation for repeated corporate misconduct cited most frequently by executives, particularly chagrined business leaders trying to explain away scandals, is that it was caused by a few "bad apples." The corporation or organization is blameless, say some; the problem is one or more individuals with a flawed ethical character who have done bad things while acting for the organization. This theory, of course, allows the executive to blame ethical failings on others: the lone employee; or perhaps Gen X, the millennials, or society or its institutions; or even employees from a foreign country or foreign subsidiary who do not share the same ethical values. In chapter 2, we assess this bad-apple theory.

ARE CORPORATE CULTURES AND INCENTIVES TO BLAME? THE BAD-BARREL THEORY

Serious misconduct, such as the VW emissions scandal described earlier in this chapter, is usually caused by something more than one or two individual employees or managers. We need to understand how corporate cultures and systems of corporate incentives and controls can lead even good employees to do wrong. The explosion of the number of ethics officers in modern corporations and the hundreds of millions of dollars spent on ethics training bring up the important question: What is going on inside corporations that cannot prevent corporate misconduct? In chapter 3, we assess this bad-barrel theory.

ARE CORRUPT COMPETITORS AND ENVIRONMENTS TO BLAME? THE BAD-ORCHARD THEORY

Some corporate executives have regarded business ethics and business responsibility professors like the two of us as hopelessly naive. They believe the only way to be successful in business is to play by the rules of the corrupt environments they face every day. And they believe most other competitors are corrupt in some way. These executives argue that they are only "leveling the playing field" and permitting their companies to compete on an equal footing. In chapter 4, we assess this bad-orchard theory. We also report on the specific efforts companies have made to control those environments or buffer themselves from the pressures to adopt the behavior of competitors.

THE CHALLENGE IS GREAT, BUT THERE IS A SOLUTION

We understand that changing corporate ethical and social behavior is a significant challenge. But we believe there are concrete steps that can be taken now to reduce corporate misconduct. These involve significant change in the behavior of corporate executives, managers and employees at all levels, policy makers, and business educators. The final three chapters of the book, chapters 5, 6, and 7, address this challenge in detail.

We don't think the vast majority of executives and employees in companies wake up in the morning with the intention of doing wrong. Instead, the various pressures both inside and outside the corporation cause them to make decisions they often regret. This book explores the real business world they live and operate in.

We recognize that making companies more ethical and responsible, thus reducing misconduct, is a complex job. But it is achievable. We don't think that all misconduct can be eliminated, but corporations, their top executives, and their boards can reduce the incidence significantly. There is an important role to play for regulators, investors, and even business ethics professors.

USE OF CASES IN THIS BOOK

Throughout the book, we document and discuss in greater depth specific examples of corporate misconduct to highlight both the breadth and depth of corporate ethical challenges and how companies have mishandled them. In all, we provide extensive details on seventeen recent major corporate scandals and invoke a number of other incidents of misconduct that help tell the story of corporate ethical failure. These various scandals affect different industries and companies of very different sizes. Some exhibit challenges related to the bad individuals; others, bad corporate cultures; and still others, bad competitive environments. Many are examples of more than one cause of misconduct.

Readers will find a more detailed discussion of Massey Energy, Peanut Corporation of America, Barings Bank, Enron, Satyam, and Theranos in chapter 2; Wells Fargo, Boeing, Takata Corporation, Blue Bell Creameries, and BP in chapter 3; and Airbus, Embraer, Rana Plaza, Equifax, and JPMorgan Chase in chapter 4. These examples, and others mentioned, help to illustrate both the challenges of and solutions to creating and sustaining ethical behavior in corporate life. They are not atypical, and the misconduct could have been avoided in each case.

Some of the examples are more detailed and are used to introduce chapters, as VW led this chapter. Others are chosen to illustrate a specific cause or potential solution. Some of these behaviors are intentional; others result from individuals being tempted by corporate incentives. Still other examples are from individuals who slid down that "slippery slope" by doing something less serious but who gradually behaved in more egregious ways. Some behaviors are legal violations; others are unethical in our view but may not be addressed by specific laws.

The companies in these examples are global. They are mostly multinational companies with operations in dozens of countries. No matter where companies are based or operate, however, examples of corporate misconduct seem to transcend national borders. The problems that we highlight are common for businesses everywhere, and the diagnoses and solutions can be applied to companies of any size.

CHAPTER 2

The Bad Apple: Bad People Do Bad Things

We begin our search for a deeper explanation of corporate misconduct by examining whether morally flawed individuals, not the companies they work for, are primarily to blame. This is the bad-apple theory.

We define a "bad apple" as an individual who cheats or misbehaves in his or her role as an employee or manager of the business. Even a good company has individuals who do wrong no matter how strongly a business discourages and penalizes their behavior. Bad apples cheat the company and its customers. Bad apples disobey company policy and ethical standards. Bad apples put the company at risk by mistreating customers, suppliers, competitors, business partners, and other employees. Bad apples are indeed at the core of many scandals.

Consider the following cases of bad apples in corporations.

Barings Bank:
A Rogue Trader Leads to Corporate Collapse

Founded in 1762, Barings Bank was the oldest merchant bank in Britain, as well as one of the largest and most stable. In 1995, the bank was single-handedly destroyed by Nick Leeson, a derivatives trader and operations manager, through unauthorized speculation in futures contracts and other dealings.

In 1992, Leeson was one of two Barings traders based in Singapore. Shortly after arriving there, he opened a special "error" account that he used for his unauthorized trading. Within a year of his arrival, he was appointed general manager and responsible for both the front office that did the trading and the back office that processed the paperwork. He reported large profits to headquarters while hiding his losses in the error account. As is often the case in situations like this, to try to recover from his losses, he made bigger and riskier bets on the market. The market kept falling, and Leeson kept losing. By 1995, his losses were S$1.4 billion (US$1 billion). He fled to Malaysia, where he wrote a book titled *Rogue Trader* that describes his fraudulent, speculative, and unauthorized activities in detail.

Leeson's futures-trading activities led to a total loss of S$2.2 billion (US$1.6 billion), as well as his conviction on fraud and forgery charges and a sentence of more than six years in prison. And they resulted in the forced takeover of a historically significant 233-year-old company by Dutch finance company ING Group. Barings was unable to meet cash requirements and was declared insolvent within a week of the discovery of Leeson's unauthorized trading losses.

A basic principle of internal controls and corporate governance was violated here by giving Leeson the responsibility of checking his own trades without adequate supervision or controls. Although such a practice is generally unwise, it can be devastating when there is a bad apple like Leeson.

Enron: Off-Books Accounts Pump Up Earnings

Another notorious case of corporate misconduct in recent years occurred at a Houston-based energy company known as Enron. From the 1980s until its devastating demise in 2001, Enron grew rapidly through a series of mergers and came to dominate the energy industry. Led by Kenneth Lay, the company was lauded as the most innovative company in America by *Fortune* magazine for six years in a row and became the seventh-largest company in the United States. At its peak, Enron was valued at $70 billion, and Lay was among the most respected corporate leaders in the United States.

Lay's strategy was to focus heavily on the energy-trading business in addition to owning some hard assets like pipelines. But as the company faced challenges, Enron tried to cover up its losses through fraudulent accounting, off-balance-sheet deceits, deceptive disclosures, and shredded documents. Enron is particularly known for its improper use of offshore-owned companies and special-purpose accounting entities. Although many others were involved, including CEO Jeff Skilling and CFO Andrew Fastow, the fraudulent activities were mostly hidden from the rest of the executive team, the

board, investors, auditors, and regulators. The board trusted
Lay and never dug into the suspicious transactions. Auditors,
customers, and employees were all convinced that this was a
highly successful company.

In 2001, Enron became the largest bankruptcy in US
history. Thousands of employees lost their jobs, investors lost
their money, the prestigious national accounting firm Arthur
Andersen went out of business, the company was charged
with fraud, and senior executives went to jail. It even led to
extensive congressional investigations and the development
of numerous additional regulations by the stock exchanges,
along with the passage of the Sarbanes-Oxley Act in 2002 to
address the serious failings in corporate governance.

But the passage of new regulations does not eliminate
the legal or ethical risks. Corporate leaders set the tone and
culture of companies through both words and actions. The
board of directors has a responsibility to provide the necessary oversight of the activities of the company and its leaders. That is particularly true when the leader is charismatic
and dominant. The board at Enron blindly followed Ken Lay's
wishes because the stock price was doing so well. As it turns
out, the company was not.

Ken Lay was a bad apple. As chairman, he had a major
impact on the company's culture and the actions of the other
senior leaders. This bad apple hired other bad apples that
contaminated the whole company. An active board could
have stopped that.

Satyam Computer Services: India's Largest Corporate Fraud

In the middle of 2008, Satyam Computer Services and its influential chairman Byrraju Ramalinga Raju were honored by the World Council for Corporate Governance. In early 2009, just six months later, the company and its senior leaders became the subject of the largest fraud investigation in India's history. Raju admitted to fabricating 70 billion rupees (US$1.5 billion) of Satyam's assets and 95 percent of the previous year's revenue. He and other senior leaders were sent to prison for seven years. Despite its record for good governance, this large, respected outsourcing firm saw its market value fall by 80 percent in twenty-four hours.

This case, often called the Enron of India, is a classic example of manipulation of earnings and fictitious accounting to fool investors and hide poor performance. It is also a classic case of a bad apple who is the company's chairman and the lack of an adequate corporate governance system that provides the necessary and effective supervision of corporate activities. Long before the confession, shareholders had expressed dissatisfaction with Raju's leadership, but the board of directors and its members failed to meet their basic responsibilities.

Not only Satyam and its shareholders suffered as a result of the fraud. PricewaterhouseCoopers was fined by the US Securities and Exchange Commission (SEC) for not performing its duties and was banned from auditing in India for two years by the Securities and Exchange Board of India.

Theranos: Fake It Until You Get Caught

One more prominent example of a bad apple in the executive suite involves Theranos, a blood testing company. Starting the company after dropping out of Stanford University at the age of nineteen, founder and CEO Elizabeth Holmes claimed that she had developed a breakthrough technology for blood testing that was of better quality and available at a lower cost. She assembled a board of directors filled with famous political leaders, including former US secretaries of state Henry Kissinger and George Shultz. By 2014, she was on the cover of *Forbes* and *Fortune*. She was a star!

But the much-hyped technology was never proven to work. Evidence was falsified, and questions were deflected. Thus, the more than a million blood tests that the company did perform were often inaccurate and placed many people's lives in jeopardy. Negative media attention mounted, and in 2018 the company, which had been valued at $9 billion, suddenly collapsed. Investors lost all their money, and founder and CEO Elizabeth Holmes faced serious legal challenges.

Holmes seemed to have lied about almost every aspect of the company. The SEC complaint charged that Holmes claimed that the company had $100 million in revenue when the actual amount was only $100,000. She claimed that the technology worked when the evidence did not support the claims. She created a culture of fear. Secrecy was mandated, and employees who dared to question the technology, quality control, or other aspects of the business were fired. Elizabeth Holmes is a bad apple. Whereas in some cases (like Enron), the bad apple seems to affect the entire barrel, at Theranos Elizabeth Holmes was dominant and controlling, so it was primarily her deeds that created the company's amazing rise and its dramatic fall. Certainly, the blame here is on this bad apple.

But the board of directors is also responsible for not doing its job of overseeing the most basic of the company's activities. The star-studded board of directors did not have many of the attributes that lead to good corporate governance. The board members had little knowledge of the technology or the operations of the business, showed little diligence, and did not ask questions to provide much strategic oversight. They did not protect the company or the investors (mostly wealthy and well-known business leaders and venture capitalists) who had invested almost a billion dollars.

It was not until a *Wall Street Journal* reporter investigated rumors of troubles at the company and one of its employees (the grandson of board member George Shultz) filled in some of the blanks that the fraud was revealed. Litigation and criminal prosecutions will likely continue for years.

Despite the prevalence of CEOs in the previous examples, there are thousands of cases of individuals far from the executive suite who have proved themselves bad apples. Bad apples falsify financial reports, embezzle money, skip safety checks, and play favorites. One of the most commonly encountered bad-apple incidents in corporations is expense-report fraud. Almost every large company has one or more bad apples who cannot resist the temptation to game the expense-reimbursement system. Many companies require extensive documentation and enforce tighter and tighter auditing to hold it in check. Most companies have established escalating penalties to weed out the most egregious bad apples, but the problem still persists.

The other most common bad-apple behavior is sexual or racial harassment. Sadly, bullying and harassment are found in almost all organizational cultures. Companies have found that some employees, perhaps because of their own feelings of inferiority or the perverse pleasure they get from dominating others, cannot resist belittling other employees, particularly women and people of color. Whereas more of this behavior was tolerated in the past, companies have recently been quicker to fire this type of bad apple.

Companies have a special concern for bad apples in middle management. They worry about individual managers or supervisors who try to pump up their own performance or the results of their department or division by falsifying financial reports, skipping required safety and quality procedures, or bribing purchasers. Sometimes middle managers who are overly anxious to advance will use their power to intimidate others. When middle-manager misconduct emerges, it reflects badly on senior management and the company for placing such a person in a position of authority and influence.

BUT ARE BAD APPLES THE PRIMARY CAUSE OF CORPORATE MISCONDUCT?

One thing should be clear to anyone who has lived in the real world: some people are good, and some people are bad. Others are basically good but are vulnerable to temptation and any incentive or pressure to do bad. Some more easily step onto the slippery slope of unethical behavior, where a small compromise leads to more and more serious behavior. Organizations have to protect themselves from the criminals and sociopaths but also from those of weak integrity who succumb more quickly to temptation or pressure.

Both good people and bad people work for companies. Every company we have ever worked with has had some bad apples! Most of us have encountered employees who cheat on their expense reports, who take home a stack of office supplies for their children, or who take credit for someone else's accomplishment. There are bad people in every type of organization. Every community, school, fraternal society, and nonprofit organization—and even every church and synagogue—has both bad people and ethically weak individuals.

Corporate executives are prone to blaming bad apples whenever a scandal arises. They have an incentive to blame *every* incident of corporate misconduct on bad apples rather than on their own actions or the company's incentives or culture. But are bad apples the *primary* or *sole* cause of the discouraging record of corporate misconduct?

Bad apples are certainly not the only cause of misconduct, but they do exist and have to be stopped if we are going to reverse the litany of corporate scandals. Companies must be concerned about the integrity of their executives and their employees. Every company's ethics and compliance group spends much of its time auditing and investigating the behavior of individual employees. In most companies, quarterly reports are submitted to the board audit committee on the number of "incidents" of individual employee misbehavior, as well as how many were disciplined and fired. If large companies were to report *no* such incidents during a quarter, it is likely they are not looking hard enough or are deliberately hiding the bad apples they found.

Are there more bad apples than in past years? Is the problem growing, or is this just how it feels? Some observers argue that society's moral compass, the commitment to ethical behavior, has collapsed in the past generation. These skeptics have pointed to the coddling of the current generation, the tolerance of drugs and sex, and the cultural fixation with promoting self-esteem. These influences, according to some, have produced a generation of narcissistic individuals who are concerned only with their own welfare and more frequently cheat their employers and take advantage of others.

Critics of modern business education blame the many cases of executive and white-collar crime on curricula that enshrine profit maximization and the pursuit of self-interest as the highest economic principles. Any notion that businesses serve a social purpose, these critics argue, has been squeezed out of students by the time they finish business school. A few critics blame the business ethics courses themselves, arguing that the courses encourage cynicism about ethics and even provide ways to rationalize self-serving behavior.

It is unclear that there are *more* bad apples today than in the past, but companies have been more diligent in uncovering and reporting the misbehaviors of individual employees. Government agencies require disclosure of incidents that violate regulatory or legal standards, and the media have access to those reports. Investigative journalism and whistleblowers make public many more incidents. Finally, companies themselves have come to believe that quick disclosure of misconduct is the most effective way to soften the blow to their reputations, and federal law gives credit for self-reporting incidents. All these factors can make it feel like the problem is getting worse, not better.

WHERE DO BAD APPLES COME FROM?

There is much debate over why some individuals are bad apples. Some "nature" advocates believe there are genetic origins of bad behavior—that some employees are inclined to be self-centered narcissists or even sociopaths. Some argue that human beings are inherently good or evil and that the worst individuals do bad with absolutely no awareness of or care for the damage and suffering they cause. There is no genetic profile of such individuals available today, so companies can't use a blood test to identify and weed them out before they are hired. Only when they misbehave within the firm can they be dealt with.

Others argue that "nurture" makes the difference—the values one learns in families, local communities, religious practice, and previous work experiences. This belief suggests that one might be able to determine whether prospective hires are bad apples by examining their background or by probing their thinking process or experiences. Some retailers give prospective employees "integrity tests" to attempt to identify those who might steal from the company. Likewise, several major business schools have used an ethics question on their application forms to help assess the integrity of applicants. A typical question reads: "Tell us about an ethical challenge you faced in your professional or personal life, how you handled it, and what you learned from it." Still, we are skeptical that one can actually measure integrity by reading such responses.

If "nurture" is the problem, is a flawed ethical character the fault of our own nurturing institutions—our families, our churches, our schools, even our civic culture? Have these done their job in instilling good values and a strong moral character in those entering the job market? Many observers argue that the American family is troubled and that parents no longer teach clear moral lessons to their children. Religious affiliation and practice have declined for a generation. The "nones" (those who respond "none" when asked about religious affiliation) are the fastest-growing religious group. Public schools have retreated from moral instruction because of the concern that they would be labeled as sectarian. Apple's first chairman, A. C. "Mike" Markkula Jr., created one of the most active applied university ethics centers in the world because of his belief that schools and colleges were producing a generation of "ethical agnostics." Finally, community and civic life has grown less respectful and compassionate, devolving into a war of competing narrow interests and rabid partisan conflicts.

While there is some truth in these criticisms, we believe that there aren't more bad people in the world now than in the past. In our decades of teaching business ethics and doing corporate consulting, we have worked with a relatively consistent population of students, executives, managers, and employees. Some are determined to put their good values to work in a business career. Most are generally well intentioned but don't really understand how much their values will be challenged; they are focused more on their own success. And a few in every class are destined to push the ethical boundaries or blow past them without a second thought.

THE ROLE OF CHARACTER

One of the primary reasons there are bad-apple scandals in business is that individuals differ in their moral strength and ethical courage. Each person has a different ability to resist pressures and temptations to cheat or violate ethical standards. What we call *moral character* is the combination of their values and their ethical strength or courage.

No two individuals have the same values. Some are focused only on their own interests and ignore the impact of their behavior on others. Some individuals seek only to enrich and pleasure themselves in the moment, sometimes failing even to seek their own long-term self-interest. These narcissists sometimes do not even understand how they hurt others or the organizations they are supposed to serve.

Most employees fall between the completely selfish and the completely selfless, between "devils" who are always angling for their own advantage and "angels" who are always seeking to serve others. Most employees try to follow the rules in business and their own general ethical sense of things. On the other hand, they might hear the company's statements about ethics and corporate responsibility, but they don't see business as a place to do good and serve others; rather, they see business solely as a place to make a living.

For some, the desires to succeed, get rich, or be a star employee are coupled with the belief that it is ethically permissible to do anything necessary to achieve their goals. They believe that the only people who get ahead in business, and life, are those willing to break the rules and push aside any who get in their way. They buy into an image of business as a dog-eat-dog world where only the strong (and paranoid) survive.

Some who give in to the temptation and pressure to cheat, we have found, have a rough but misguided standard of justice. "I have been cheated out of a promotion," some will rationalize, and therefore they believe it is OK for them to cheat the company in some way to compensate. Others describe their own misconduct as simply leveling the playing field against others who do not play fair.

Beyond basic value differences, two types of impaired or faulty decision-making are common. Some in business simply are not capable of empathy—specifically in terms of understanding how their decisions or those of their company will affect others. They don't comprehend the impact on customers, suppliers, or even fellow employees and are not capable of considering it. Among these are some who are simply not capable of the cognitive work that would identify these impacts.

Ethical strength and courage are also present in varying degrees. There are many individuals who do not have confidence in their own ethical judgment. They may defer too quickly to the pressure to conform or participate actively in misconduct. The less confident personality is also more likely to cover up a mistake or misdeed rather than face it head-on. The cover-up, not telling the truth or disclosing what has happened, becomes a bigger ethical problem.

Personal moral strength appears to follow a normal distribution (i.e., a bell curve) in any group of employees. Some individuals' values and weaknesses of character make them more likely to misbehave. Other individuals have such strong values and character that they will not cheat or violate company policy no matter what the circumstance. Most employees fall somewhere in between. They have good values and would like to do the right thing, but they are susceptible to greater or lesser pressure to cheat or to solve a personal financial crisis by stealing or taking a bribe. Managing ethically diverse and imperfect employees is an unavoidable task of corporate management.

There is considerable debate about whether individuals who are caught up in corrupt corporate cultures and succumb to their pressures are inherently bad people or are good people caught in a toxic environment. Many scandals result from one or a few bad apples who create a bad culture, which in turn ensnares individuals with weak moral character in the scandals. As the Wells Fargo case in the next chapter illustrates, a culture can be so strong that it causes hundreds and even thousands of normal employees to do wrong. But individuals whose ethical strength is weak may succumb to even the mildest incentives to cut an ethical corner. Companies can reduce the likelihood that an ethically weak individual will become a bad apple by strengthening the corporate culture and reinforcing its signals that the company expects only the most ethical behavior from its employees.

HOW DO BAD APPLES DAMAGE THE COMPANY?

Bad apples can do tremendous damage to the company and to its reputation. The actions of a single bad apple can destroy the company itself, as the example of Nick Leeson earlier in this chapter illustrated. Because of a bad apple in the executive suite, Enron ceased to exist as a company, and the participation of Arthur Andersen accountants led to that firm's demise as well.

Bad apples can disrupt the personal and financial lives of their organization's customers, employees, and business partners. They can hold back the careers of any individual who was working for the company at the time. Mere association with companies that have had prominent scandals can make it hard for employees or business partners to get their next job.

Bad apples can indeed harm more than their employees and investors, too. They can be directly responsible for the deaths of a few, or even many. Consider the following two cases.

Massey Energy Mines: Safety Violations Lead to Miner Deaths

In 2010, tragedy struck when twenty-nine miners died in an explosion at a Massey Energy–owned mine in West Virginia after improper ventilation allowed gases to accumulate. The company was the nation's fourth-largest coal company. The explosion was the worst mining disaster in forty years.

CEO Don Blankenship, once one of the most powerful men in the region, was convicted of conspiring to violate federal safety standards and sent to prison. Prosecutors had argued that the company established a culture that was focused solely on profits and that Blankenship's leadership was responsible for the catastrophe.

"Employees were to ignore safety standards and practices if they threatened profits," according to the prosecutors. Even while there were increasing safety problems at the mine, the focus remained on increasing production and the company's stock price, which closely tracked Blankenship's own personal wealth. The company covered up safety violations and deceived both regulators and shareholders. There was evidence that the company manipulated the ventilation system, hid safety violations during inspections to fool safety inspectors, falsified coal dust samples, and warned miners before surprise visits so that any violations could be hidden. A superintendent at the company said that more than a hundred employees were part of an advance-warning system to signal the arrival of inspectors.

In addition to issues of criminal and civil fraud and negligence, the tragedy highlighted a corporate governance failure. Don Blankenship had the dual role of CEO and chairman, which certainly compromised the board's oversight function. He was also dictatorial and constantly chastised subordinates. The company had thousands of safety citations and little activity to address them.

With a dominant leader like Blankenship or Ken Lay, it is critical that an active board of directors fulfills its ethical and legal responsibilities to provide independent and ethical oversight. That was not done. The New York state comptroller argued that "this tragedy was a failure both of risk management and effective board oversight."

Peanut Corporation of America: *Salmonella* Outbreak

In 2015, Stewart Parnell, the CEO of the now-closed Peanut Corporation of America, received a twenty-eight-year prison sentence after being convicted of seventy-two counts of fraud and conspiracy for his role in a 2008 *Salmonella* outbreak, which resulted in nine deaths and 714 cases of infections. Others related to the case were also given lengthy sentences, including Parnell's brother, two plant managers, and a quality-assurance manager. These were the first federal felony convictions related to food poisoning, and the case involved the most extensive food recall in US history.

Employees and federal inspectors found roaches, rats, bird droppings, a leaky roof, and more in the Georgia and Texas facilities during their investigation. The *Salmonella* outbreak forced over 360 companies to recall more than 3,900 peanut products in forty-six states. Schools had to pull their tainted lunch products, food banks had to discard thousands of pounds of sustenance intended for those in need, and the Federal Emergency Management Agency (FEMA) had to recall emergency meals. The estimated losses in the peanut industry were more than $1 billion.

Although there were problems throughout the company, the misconduct was led by the CEO and a few key leaders. These bad apples were more focused on short-term profits than the welfare of their employees and customers. When Parnell was told that a shipment was delayed because they were waiting for *Salmonella* test results, his response was "Just ship it."

The company filed for bankruptcy in 2009 and ceased all operations. This should provide caution to corporate leaders as to the potential consequences of poor and unethical business practices. It is an example of poor management control systems, lax enforcement, and more concern for short-term profits than customer and employee safety.

―――――――――――――――――――

As noted before, bad apples don't need to be CEOs to wreak considerable havoc. A single employee who skips a production step or quality test and ships a contaminated product can harm hundreds of millions of users and create the public belief that all the company's products are tainted. Chipotle was extremely slow to recover from the damage to its reputation caused by food poisonings that apparently resulted from poor food-safety practices in some of its restaurants. The divisional executive or branch manager who falsifies a market survey or quarterly financial report to make his or her own performance look better can cost the company substantial amounts of money due to flawed decisions made on the basis of that falsified report. And these isolated incidents of misreporting can create skepticism about all the company's financial reports and the capability of management, possibly resulting in a drop in stock price.

PREDICTING WHICH EMPLOYEES WILL BE BAD APPLES

It would be very useful to be able to identify bad apples before they misbehave and embroil the company in a scandal. Exhibit 2-1 summarizes some of the signs of moral weakness described in the previous pages. These are seen as either leading indicators to or the direct cause of misconduct and scandals.

A common signal is a narcissistic personality. Some executives, managers, and employees are focused on nothing beyond how a situation affects them personally—how it will help them get promoted, be seen as the star, or earn the biggest bonus. Too often, such individuals will do anything to serve their own needs, including violating legal rules, company policies, and ethical norms. Narcissistic individuals lack empathy, which would help them understand how their actions will affect others. This can cause them to engage in misconduct because they do not realize that it affects others negatively.

Making ethical decisions requires cognitive skill as well. Some individuals lack the ability to see how a general rule or ethical principle translates to the specific decision they are making. Others are simply overwhelmed by the complexity and speed of modern business.

Some individuals simply have a weaker moral character than others. Signs of a weak moral character include the tendency to give in to pressure or seek the easy or expedient way out of difficult situations. Moral character seems to be partly innate, perhaps even genetic, and partly shaped by families, churches, and personal experiences. Individuals who have practiced ethical courage

EXHIBIT 2-1

INDICATIONS OF MORAL WEAKNESS
OR VULNERABILITY IN EMPLOYEES

1. **Narcissistic personal values**: belief that "how I am affected is all that matters"
2. **Lack of empathy**: inability to consider or be concerned about how others are affected
3. **Cognitive limitation**: lack of understanding that a rule applies to a certain case
4. **Difficulty handling the speed of modern business**: results in less time for reflection
5. **Weakness of moral character**: tendency to give in to temptation or pressure
6. **Weakness of personality**: difficulty standing up to others
7. **Embarrassment**: a desire to cover up one's own mistakes and misconduct
8. **Pattern of petty dishonesty and deception**: displays pattern at work or at home; includes past criminal behavior
9. **Personal financial difficulty**: particularly when it results from overspending
10. **Belief that you only get ahead in business by stretching the rules**

before—standing up for what is right—are more likely to do what is right under pressures or incentives to do wrong.

Some employees are simply intimidated by supervisors and managers, more likely to do whatever they are told, and more likely to cover up situations where they cannot meet a supervisor's expectations. These employees can be quicker to succumb to pressure from a boss to falsify a report or ship a substandard product to improve a division's earnings. Other weak personalities can find

it impossible to resist lax systems, and so they act on small temptations. Individuals of weaker moral character find it particularly
hard to do courageous things such as reporting the misconduct of
others or challenging their bosses.

Every company struggles with whether to take past bad behavior or behavior in one's personal life as a sign that a person is
more likely to be a bad apple at work in the future. Past criminal
behavior can give valid indications of a person's moral weakness or
narcissism. So can noncriminal discipline, such as being expelled
from college or being fired from a previous job. But should a single
incident of misconduct disqualify a person from employment or
result in termination? Does a person's serial infidelity in marriages
indicate a tendency to be a bad apple at work? Patterns of repeated
behavior or lack of remorse are more likely to raise the risk that a
person will behave badly again.

Some bad apples are caused by pressures in the employee's
private life. That pressure can be financial; they steal to make the
rent, to pay for unexpected medical bills, or to meet their spouse's
expectation of certain comforts. The pressure can also be personal,
perhaps the employee's sense of personal failure or the demands of
a spouse or extended family to be more successful. The wise manager offers support quickly when such pressures are known.

Finally, some employees come to believe that acting unethically, at least at times, is necessary to get ahead. They argue that
this "law of the jungle" is the way the world works. Companies
can usually detect the employees who are overly competitive with
people inside the company or engage in gossip to "take down" their
own bosses in order to get ahead.

Any of these causes can lead individuals to cut corners, falsify
reports, hide their own failures, or steal from the firm. When those
of weaker moral character compromise their values once, perhaps

in a small matter like padding an expense report, the next violation becomes easier. The slippery slope is real. Many bad apples started small and then cascaded into larger and larger misconduct.

Some employees, of course, see their work in idealistic terms, as a chance to create products and services that both meet people's needs and solve social problems. In launching the Business Enterprise Trust awards for individual business integrity in 1988, television pioneer Norman Lear argued that these moral exemplars could bring a resurgence of values to American and global business. He worried that the four traditional pillars of our American culture—family, church, school, and civic culture—were all failing to shape the values of youth.

HOW COMPANIES MANAGE GOOD AND BAD APPLES

Managing bad apples is a critical task in any firm that seeks to avoid misconduct. How do companies reduce this risk?

As some executives we have worked with emphasize, the challenge in dealing with both the good and bad apples in any organization addresses three key capabilities:

1. The company must avoid hiring ethically weak individuals as much as possible.
2. The company must uncover bad behaviors of individuals as quickly as possible, reducing the damage they do and firing them if warranted.
3. The company must strengthen the incentives to do the right thing.

HIRING

Hiring managers can predict with some accuracy the likelihood that an individual will become a bad apple through an overall evaluation of how they talk about themselves, their personal aspirations, their extracurricular activities, what they report they have learned from prior experience, and the incidence of integrity questions in their career to date. Individuals who think naturally and deeply about the impact of their behavior on others and about the fairness of policies are likely to be on the positive end of the integrity distribution.

Most often, hiring managers are engaged in the kind of overall assessment of the values of job candidates we mentioned before. If candidates demonstrate concern for the many individuals they have worked with, for the interests of their former employer, for the social and ethical impact of their own and their company's work, then they are more likely to fall on the positive end of the integrity spectrum. If they talk only about themselves, about the financial aspects of their employment, about the opportunities to get ahead, one should be concerned and probe more deeply. Similarly, how candidates describe their previous experience, particularly why they left jobs or the meaning of gaps in their employment, can give hints about their ability to face up to embarrassment, temptation, and pressure.

Occasionally an employer interviews a candidate who has either been implicated in a prior scandal or worked at a company that had a major scandal, such as Massey Energy or Theranos. In those cases, an employer can gain information by asking the candidate to describe their own role, what they were aware of, and how they handled themselves during the scandal. Even in the case of individuals who have not been implicated in a scandal, a general question about the culture and values of the former employer can give useful information. A candidate who praises the "take no prisoners" culture of a former employer might raise red flags, as would hints that no one had to work very hard at the candidate's previous job.

Not all companies ask the questions we recommend. Our experience with companies suggests, instead, that hiring managers are often impressed by the overly confident and aggressive applicant, who may actually represent a higher risk of being a bad apple.

DETECTING THE BAD APPLE

If bad apples are inevitable in all organizations, then one of the most important things a company can do is build the capacity to identify bad behavior quickly and stop it. An employee's direct supervisor is the most important individual in controlling the behavior of the bad apple. The direct supervisor—whether a first-line supervisor of an hourly employee, or a CEO whose direct report is a senior vice president—will be the first to see patterns that should raise concerns. A sloppy or falsified expense report; harsh words to a colleague or subordinate; the tendency to skate "close to the edge" in meeting regulations, internal corporate policies, or even performance goals—all are early signs of ethical weakness and risk.

To identify the situations warranting early intervention, however, the company needs the systems to bring the behavior to the attention of the direct supervisor and the attentiveness of the supervisor to patterns that are apparent from multiple reports and observation. Unfortunately, direct supervisors vary greatly in their attentiveness and their skill in handling early indications of questionable behavior. They even vary greatly in their own ethics, including whether they think what the employee has done is wrong. In some cases, the direct supervisor has been the one to demand that the employee engage in the questionable behavior.

Notably, the better the employee's performance is, by the standards of productivity, sales, or profit return, the less likely a direct supervisor is to intervene early when signs of ethical trouble arise. The direct supervisor has a stake in the good performance of the employee and tends to think the ethical flags are isolated or overstated. Our experience has shown us that early intervention can both avoid some subsequent misbehavior and "save" a productive employee who might have had to be fired later. Coaching and mild penalties for first offenses can be accompanied by clear communication that "we don't do things like that around here" and that a reoccurrence will lead to serious discipline or firing.

As noted earlier in this chapter, there are indications of weak moral character in individuals. When they have not prevented the hiring of a potential bad apple, the same indicators can help the supervisor or manager identify a problem employee earlier rather than later.

STRENGTHENING THE INCENTIVES TO DO THE RIGHT THING

Creating an ethical corporate culture is the topic of the next chapter, but several key strategies for doing so are critical to managing the potential bad apples in the firm.

A significant amount of **signaling** takes place in the hiring and orientation of new employees. While most firms inform applicants that the company has an ethics code and perhaps include an introduction to or training on the code in orientation, new hires get much more accurate information from how the individual managers and executives they meet talk about the business and what is expected of employees. One organization may have a highly hierarchical culture, where one is expected to do what the boss says and where resisting a boss is difficult. This can raise the likelihood that the new employee will "go along" rather than question practices and decisions. Another company may have created an open culture in which asking questions and challenging supervisors is encouraged.

By contrast, companies can signal other things about the culture that reinforce the likelihood that a new employee will do the right thing. Among these are communicating a strong commitment to ethical behavior, a basic respect for the views of all employees, the desire to hear the perspectives and input of all employees, and the importance of helping the company live the ethical values written into the mission and values statements and codes of conduct.

In managing the individual employee, and the bad apples among these employees, **systems and policies** are critical. While we believe compliance has been overemphasized relative to ethics in much corporate management, every company needs an effective set of compliance policies and systems. The individual employee must know what kinds of behavior are expected and be aware that an effective monitoring or auditing system will catch deviations from that behavior.

Perhaps the most controversial aspect of identifying a potential bad apple is judging the past behaviors of individuals. Dishonesty on petty matters, such as expense-report cheating, claiming credit for others' work, and failure to keep their supervisors informed of problems in their own areas of responsibility, should alert managers of possible problems. So should patterns of petty or serious ethical problems in an individual's private life. One's character is usually made clear in the tendency to misbehave on the job and also in private life. Individuals who tend to cheat on their life partners, tell racist or sexist jokes, find ways to claim discounts they do not qualify for, or praise such behavior should alert a manager to a problem.

SO, ARE BAD APPLES THE CAUSE OF CORPORATE MISCONDUCT?

At this point, we have examined only one of the potential explanations for the continuing pattern of corporate misconduct, the bad apple. We believe every organization has its bad apples, and they do real damage. We also believe that their destructive effects can often be avoided by good hiring practices and early detection.

Many employees who misbehave are good people or average people caught up in bad cultures. The quality of the corporate culture can enable or discourage the bad apple. Therefore, we turn next to examining the contribution made by bad or weak corporate cultures.

CHAPTER 3

The Bad Barrel: Toxic Company Cultures Encourage Misconduct

A bad barrel is a corporate culture that tolerates or even encourages employees violating legal or ethical norms. It may incentivize the employees who work there to cut corners, violate legal and regulatory standards, and sometimes treat classes of employees or customers with disrespect or outright hostility.

We have all experienced dysfunctional cultures at some point in our lives—in a company or work group where some or all employees are treated poorly, in a community that is racist or discriminatory toward one ethnic group or another, or even in a family that is characterized more by attacks on one another than by love. Some organizational and social cultures were toxic from their earliest days; others go bad over time.

Any employee who has worked for more than one company can tell you that corporate cultures really do differ. Some companies treat their employees, customers, suppliers, and the community much better than others. But other cultures communicate openly that it's only about making money and favoring an in-group that controls the business. Some companies encourage employees to think about their work as serving the real need of individuals and society, what has come to be called corporate "purpose." Others encourage employees to do anything necessary to "meet the numbers." In a few, the message is "don't tell me how you did it" or "don't give me excuses; just get it done."

Consider the following cases of dysfunctional corporate cultures.

Wells Fargo: Sham Customer Accounts

In 2016, Wells Fargo announced that it had fired 5,300 managers and other employees for "engaging in improper sales practices" over the previous five years. This fraudulent activity led to a $185 million penalty, the largest fine in the brief history of the US Consumer Financial Protection Bureau. Yet, the same cross-selling focus at the core of the scandal had also led the company to an industry-topping profitability rate, for which the CEO won the 2013 Banker of the Year award.

The US House and Senate hearings at the time were unusually critical of the company's actions, with charges of "gutless leadership" and calls for CEO John Stumpf's resignation and a criminal investigation. Congressman Brad Sherman told Stumpf, "You took 5,300 good Americans and turned them into felons." Senator Pat Toomey declared, "This isn't cross selling, its fraud."

The cross-selling tactic in question involved offering customers the option to open, and at times pressuring them to open, additional accounts whenever they called the bank with a question about an existing account. Trying to sell additional products and services to existing customers is a common sales practice, but Wells Fargo, one of the largest banks in the world, pushed it beyond all reasonable limits. Between 2011 and 2016, Wells Fargo employees had opened two million customer accounts without the customers' knowledge or permission. The employees transferred funds from customer accounts without permission to fund the new accounts and also created fake email addresses for confirmation.

Wells Fargo had promoted cross-selling to increase sales and profitability and had aligned employee incentives and pay based in part on how many products were sold. Not surprisingly, sales employees pressured customers to open new accounts and even went to family and friends to open unneeded accounts to achieve sales quotas. Managers certainly did not discourage these tactics and sometimes encouraged them. Employees' sales goals were raised several times and were divided into daily and even hourly goals, further increasing the pressure on the employees.

Furthermore, because the incentives were related only to the opening of new accounts, employees began to open accounts without authorization from customers, planning to close them shortly thereafter. The practice spread rapidly across Wells Fargo's sales operations. More and more unauthorized accounts were left open, accruing fees to the customers.

Cross-selling was a key component of Wells Fargo's strategy—focusing on selling more products to existing customers rather than devoting resources to recruiting new customers—and the rewards to employees were aligned with that strategy. The company's profitability and stock performance reflected the success of that tactic. The problem was, and often is, that this success was achieved through the use of unethical and often illegal means that were encouraged by senior executives.

The costs to Wells Fargo have grown since that initial $185 million fine. Legal fees continue to mount, related to federal and state investigations; class-action lawsuits; and various other lawsuits from employees, customers, and regulators. Numerous business and government bank customers have refused to do business with the bank because of these activities.

As with many other cases, this very public scandal may be part of a pattern of behavior rather than a onetime event. Here are a few other examples of recent misbehavior at Wells Fargo: In a 2008 case on a Wells Fargo foreclosure, Bankruptcy Judge Elizabeth Magner condemned the company's "abusive imposition of unwarranted fees and charges." In a 2010 case, Bankruptcy Judge Jeff Bohm said, "When mistakes happen not once, not twice, but repeatedly and when actions are not taken to correct these mistakes within a reasonable period of time, the failure to right the wrong . . . the excuse of 'mistakes happen' has no credence." And in a 2013 case, US District Judge William Young said that "the disconnect between Wells Fargo's publicly advertised face and its actual litigation conduct here could not be more extreme. A quick visit to Wells Fargo's website confirms that it vigorously promotes itself as consumer-friendly, a far cry from the hard-nosed win-at-any-cost stance it has adopted here."

What does it say about a company that has more than five thousand employees who violated these statements and mistreated its customers? It is certainly evidence of both poor oversight and controls from the company leadership and poor corporate governance on the part of the board. It also reflects a corporate culture that is more concerned about short-term corporate profits than about the benefits to customers and employees and the long-term interests of shareholders.

When the company fired employees who created fictitious and unauthorized accounts over a five-year period for "engaging in improper sales practices," why didn't company executives fix the incentive system and correct the cross-selling program at the same time? Because it was profitable. Most customers were not aware that new accounts had been opened in their name or assumed they had authorized them. In any case, they continued to pay fees on the accounts. The culture and the ethical and legal responsibilities should have been addressed years before the company was caught. This is evidence of poor oversight and regulatory controls and a lack of responsibility of the leadership and the board.

CEO John Stumpf blamed the misconduct on "a few bad apples." But thousands of mid- and lower-level employees were fired for these activities. It is hard to argue that the company had mistakenly hired more than 5,300 bad apples. Something more systemic was clearly going on. This was clearly a bad barrel—with a CEO trying to blame the employees for a culture, company leadership, and an incentive system that focused more on short-term profits than on act-ing ethically and legally.

Blue Bell Creameries: Culture of Neglect for Product Quality

In 2015, Blue Bell Creameries (a one-hundred-year-old Texas-based company and the third-largest ice-cream maker in the United States) admitted that its products caused at least ten *Listeria* infections and three deaths, forcing a production shutdown and product recall.

Although accidents do happen, this should not have been a total surprise. There was evidence that *Listeria* had been found in the company's facilities at least two years earlier and had caused sicknesses at that time. The US Food and Drug Administration (FDA) investigation found that Blue Bell did not follow up or take steps to solve the problems that had been found earlier. The Centers for Disease Control and Prevention (CDC) determined that the *Listeria* outbreak had actually begun in 2010. There were five limited recalls that did not fix the issues and ultimately led to the full recall and the financial disaster that occurred.

The infections and deaths also resulted in a criminal investigation by the US Department of Justice of the company executives' handling of the outbreak. It was clear that the company was slow to act and did not address the management-system failures, quality-control issues, or product recall as swiftly as was needed. The result was deaths, damage to Blue Bell's reputation, and significant financial loss.

Examining why the lax corporate culture for product safety could persist, the Delaware Supreme Court found that Blue Bell did not have board-level controls "ensuring that the only product it makes—ice cream—is safe to eat." Although the *Listeria* outbreak was not intentional, the company clearly did not have adequate governance, management systems, or ethical practices in place to prevent the contamination. In addition, the response to the crisis, which is often called *ethics creep* or *recall creep*, too often leads to disastrous results.

These Blue Bell failures of systems and ethics led to significant harm to both society and the company. This is an example of a bad barrel with multiple causes: board neglect, inadequate leadership, and employee disregard. Neither the board nor the leadership understood that they were not even serving the narrow interests of the shareholders, given the powerful connection between producing a safe product and long-term corporate profitability.

Takata Corporation: Airbags That Kill, Not Protect

Another example of how a quest for reduced costs results in decisions that have enormous consequences for individuals, society, and companies is the Japanese firm Takata Corporation, which in 2015 found itself at the center of a controversy over the manufacturing of dangerous automobile airbags because of decisions to cut costs. "Happy Manipulating" is what one Takata engineer wrote in 2006 in reference to the continuing manipulation of airbag test results that had been going on since at least 2000.

Takata is an eighty-seven-year-old Japanese company that manufactures airbags and other parts sold to automobile manufacturers. In addition to the more recent problems, Takata is well known for a huge 1995 recall of millions of defective seat belts that it made for Japanese auto manufacturers. The severity of skimping on safety in its products was not new to Takata. In the seat-belt recall, the US National Highway Traffic Safety Administration (NHTSA) assessed civil penalties against both Honda and Takata after determining that the hazard was known for at least five years before any action was taken.

But the seat-belt recall, involving millions of vehicles, was small compared to the airbag recall and the damage these products did. In some cases, the airbags Takata provided to automobile manufacturers all over the world blew metal fragments toward passengers when the bags deployed in an accident. At least twenty-two deaths and hundreds of injuries are attributed to the Takata airbags. Over forty-two million cars with the airbags have been recalled for repair or replacement, constituting the largest auto recall in US history. The largest financial penalties in the NHTSA's history were assessed, and Takata filed for bankruptcy in 2017.

The problem was related to a fundamental design flaw, but the real cause was money. The airbags were filled with gas created by a propellant rather than air. A propellant engineer at Takata testified that when the company switched to ammonium nitrate as a core element of the airbags, there were many safety concerns. Although the cost of ammonium nitrate was about 90 percent lower than that of alternatives, other airbag manufacturers were not willing to use it. The engineer suggested that "somebody will be killed," but the company ignored his warnings and told him that "the decision has already been made."

The first incident of driver injury from the airbags occurred as early as 2004, but it was not until 2015 that Takata acknowledged that the problem was widespread and started to dramatically increase the number of recalled vehicles. An NHTSA spokesman said that "Takata provided inaccurate, incomplete, and misleading information to regulators for nearly a decade." Evidence provided during investigations proved that Takata knew by 1999 that the airbags could be deadly. The investigations also found that Takata falsified data, subverted testing procedures, and concealed reports that the airbags were prone to failure.

All the evidence combined indicates what a US Senate committee called "a broken safety culture" at the company. Just like with the seat belts, the airbag issue was serious for many years before anything was done about it. This failure to act on the widespread knowledge that the product was dangerous indicates the company had been a bad barrel for a long time. The systems, the culture, and the governance were focused on costs and profits, with little concern for the safety of tens of millions of customers.

Breakdowns in culture like what happened at Wells Fargo, Blue Bell, or Takata are not isolated incidents. Most corporations believe the company exists for the shareholders alone; only a very few embrace genuine concern for a broader set of stakeholders.

Some corporations even operate as if the company exists only to benefit a small group of top executives, increasing their salaries and bonuses. Some cultures tolerate misconduct of all kinds, while others constantly remind employees to meet legal obligations and uphold ethical standards.

In short, there are good and bad cultures, just as there are good and bad employees. Good and bad cultures may even be distributed on a "normal" curve, such as we proposed for individuals in the last chapter—some are almost guaranteed to violate the law and provoke scandals, and a few are immune to scandals because these companies always "do the right thing." Most companies, we suspect, are somewhere in the middle—at times walking the edge of misconduct and at other times resistant to pressures to cut corners. We also suspect that most large companies have individual units or teams that are prone to misconduct.

In recent years, more and more observers realize that corporate culture matters. Companies spend millions of dollars attempting to clearly communicate corporate values and have them reflected in the corporate culture. Prosecutors and judges are authorized to take corporate cultures into account when they decide whether to charge an individual or a company with a crime and when setting a fine for corporate wrongdoing. If a company has a serious ethics program and is known for having a culture that genuinely reinforces doing the right thing, prosecutors and judges can give the company the benefit of the doubt and conclude that an individual, or "bad apple," is responsible for misconduct.

Corporate executives, however, are much too quick to blame scandals on bad apples. In 2016, when Wells Fargo announced that it had fired thousands of employees for fraud in cross-selling over the previous five years, the company tried to blame the whole scandal on thousands of "bad apples." But at every level, Wells

Fargo's management had pushed cross-selling to increase sales and profitability and aligned employee incentives and pay based in part on how many additional products were sold to existing customers. The intensity of these incentives created a toxic culture in the sales organization that enveloped thousands of employees. Managers set the stage for the individual misconduct that followed, and they looked the other way for as long as they could.

WHERE DO BAD BARRELS COME FROM?

Every corporation, even every small business, has a culture. The culture is the unwritten ways of doing things. There is a culture in a two-person organization as well as in an organization with a hundred thousand employees. A larger organization may have multiple cultures—influenced by local managers and even by an immediate supervisor of a work team.

Cultures grow over time by the influence of many factors, including the behavior of leaders and other high-profile employees, as well as the behaviors leaders tolerate or reward in rank-and-file employees. In companies with bad cultures, ethics programs have often long existed but are not taken seriously by management. Sometimes they are even met with open hostility and derision. When new management takes charge of a company, it can be very difficult to change the toxic culture.

Bad cultures tolerate different types of bad behavior. We hear a lot about racist and misogynist cultures in the news today—where minority and female employees are harassed and systematically held back from advancement. Many bad cultures focus exclusively on quarterly goals and tend to reward sales and profits no matter how they are achieved. This leads to a disregard for the interests of customers, suppliers, and business partners.

A company's strategy and systems can give a number of signals on how the business of the company is to be conducted, influencing its culture significantly. How does an airline, for example, trade off care for passengers and their flying experience with measures to shrink seats, cut food costs, and make changes in plans difficult and expensive? On one airline, employees may be friendly, available, and genuinely helpful. On another, employees may hide out in in-flight kitchens, resentful when their reading is interrupted. These behaviors can be the direct result of a corporate culture, of a "good" or "bad" barrel.

A bad barrel can also develop when a company or its leaders openly disdain some social value, particularly values embodied in laws and regulations. In some organizations, diversity and environmental goals are openly ridiculed, and government regulations promoting them are frequently ignored.

A company does not need to take specific actions to make itself a bad barrel. Some organizations become bad barrels slowly over time. A company that talks incessantly about profitability or growth and never talks about any other goals can gradually become a bad barrel through indirect encouragement. A toxic culture can also accumulate from many small incidents and behaviors. If the CEO is abusive or belittles people, then abusive behavior spreads down through the organization. If the star salesperson can fudge on their expense reports because they bring in so much business, others get the message that the only thing that matters is results.

Every time an employee or executive is promoted, messages are sent to the organization regarding what behaviors are valued. Some companies make heroes of employees who find ways of making sales or profits in questionable ways. If employees in a company cut corners and don't get caught, they are sometimes considered "clever" or "creative." If employees in a bad culture lie or fudge numbers to help the work group or division, they may be hailed as a "real team player." Conversely, the employee who insists that the company must follow the rules may be derided as not being a team player or for being disruptive. A company that retaliates against a whistleblower or a person who advocates for better treatment of customers, other employees, or business partners sends an unmistakable message to the rest of its employees.

Cultures are strongly influenced by critical incidents in the company's history. How a highly visible decision is made sets a standard for how decisions in general are to be handled and whether a particular behavior will be tolerated. In the Massey Energy case in the preceding chapter, the combativeness of the bad-apple CEO toward regulators and gross violations of safety rules gave a clear indication that safety was not an important goal and created a bad culture in its wake. A frequently cited counter-story, which may or may not be real, describes a Nordstrom manager who took back a set of automobile tires returned by a customer who insisted he had bought them at Nordstrom. The retailer has never sold tires, but in the story, management praises the manager for his commitment to top customer service. The story reinforces the message that Nordstrom managers are supposed to go out of their way to serve customers. Bad barrels may also develop in companies that tolerate what some might consider insignificant misconduct—cutting "trivial" corners in safety or environmental testing, fudging financial numbers or regulatory reports, "harmless" cheating on expense reports. This can create a disdain or disregard for rules in general. Which can then escalate into more egregious behavior because of the effects of the slippery slope.

Most companies do not become bad barrels deliberately. They may have a set of assumed but unexamined beliefs—perhaps that business is a harsh world and that you have to be "tough" and ruthless to succeed. It may be due to a series of small but damaging decisions to tolerate behaviors to meet quarterly goals. Some executives are genuinely surprised by the bad behavior later uncovered in their own firms, unaware that they have encouraged it.

The ideology of a company's executive team can have a major impact on the corporate culture. Some executives believe that the sole purpose of the corporation is to increase its shareholders' wealth and that they are being virtuous when they resist regulation, refuse to consider any stakeholder other than shareholders, and cut salaries and employee benefits as much as possible. Other executives believe a business should have a purpose beyond making money for its investors. These attitudes filter down to all employees as they seek to emulate those values in their own ways. Ideology can cause some executives to have short-term orientations, allowing them to neglect any long-term consequences of corporate behavior, for example, to the environment or even to the firm's own survival. Others, who do not expect to be caught, tolerate questionable behavior in order to reap the immediate rewards.

Some corporate leaders are deliberate about shaping their cultures, adopting corporate values that are reinforced in frequent written and oral messages. Some efforts to create a good culture are genuine and effective, whereas others are hypocritical or often just ill-conceived. In some companies, it is understood that the values espoused in a company ethics code or values statement are purely for external consumption and do not represent how employees are actually expected to act.

Cultures are long-lasting. Bad policies and practices and "ways of doing things" can become so ingrained that it is difficult to root them out. New management brought aboard in the aftermath of a major scandal often finds it impossible to prevent further abuse and misconduct. Employees often don't know any other way of acting, of meeting their performance goals, or of making the thousands of necessary decisions per day in any large corporation.

Bad barrels can also result from neglect of good governance. Many corporate scandals have resulted from the failure of the board to impose any accountability on the organization. In the absence of any board attention, the corporate culture can go bad over a long period of time. Such a board is awakened only when a major scandal occurs, as in the cases of Blue Bell Creameries or Enron.

Strong corporate cultures take years to create and very little time to destroy. Johnson & Johnson, the medical products and pharmaceuticals firm, was hailed in the 1980s and '90s for its ethical culture and exemplary behavior in protecting customers from a madman who poisoned bottles of Tylenol. Its "credo" of corporate values, originally adopted in the 1940s, served as the lynchpin of its ethical corporate culture. Yet from 2000 on, Johnson & Johnson experienced a series of corporate scandals regarding aggressive sales practices, off-label promotions, and tainted products, and some critics now say there is little of the "old J&J culture" left.

HOW DO BAD BARRELS DAMAGE THE COMPANY?

As a customer, it is immediately apparent when you have encountered a "bad barrel." You have trouble getting in touch with the company, or if you do, you are treated poorly, sometimes with open disdain. Errors are not corrected or are remedied only when you have escalated things to the CEO or sought the help of a media consumer advocate. It may be an insurance company that always rejects a claim the first time it is made, or perhaps a company that holds large numbers of employees below twenty hours a week so that they do not qualify for benefits. As a supplier or business partner, you always seem to come in second to the other interests. You suspect that they are deliberately challenging every billing and delaying payments.

Bad treatment leads customers and suppliers to avoid doing business with that firm if they can do so. Some people have an airline they avoid if at all possible as a result of bad service in the past. Some suppliers and business partners raise their prices for particular companies to compensate for the slow bill paying or additional hassles they know they will face. The stain on a company's reputation can be costly and long-lasting.

A good corporate culture works in reverse. If customers have a good experience with a retailer, a mechanic they know is honest, or a platform they believe genuinely protects the privacy of their data, they will do business with that company again and again.

Bad barrels that treat employees poorly can find it challenging to hire the best people. Employees who feel mistreated are also less loyal and less productive, and they leave more readily for other opportunities. High turnover raises the costs of doing business. Unhappy employees may also feel justified in "ripping off the company," as in taking office supplies home or cheating on expense reports.

Bad barrels sometimes encourage their employees to skip required steps or disobey regulations, as long as they do not get caught, thereby increasing the number of violations. Companies that are frequent violators of regulations may then be targeted by regulators for tighter enforcement and heavier penalties. Such companies may also see an increase in whistleblowers, including employees who go outside the firm's reporting system to win whistleblower financial rewards when available.

Two additional cases can help us see patterns that slowly created a bad culture and eventually disaster: Boeing and BP.

Boeing: New Software Leads to 737 MAX Crashes

The crashes of two Boeing 737 MAX airplanes in 2018 and 2019 caused the deaths of 346 people. After the second crash, many concluded that the two crashes were related and that Boeing knew about the technical problems for some time before the crashes, took no action, and was responsible. Aviation authorities worldwide proceeded to ground all the MAX planes after the second crash in March 2019.

Later, some observers suggested that the 2009 crash of an earlier Boeing 737 model in Amsterdam that caused ten deaths might be related. Experts view both the causes and Boeing's response to the 2009 crash as failures of responsibility and similar to the later crashes. But the question lingered of whether the technical failure was due to the actions of a single employee, a bad apple, or was encouraged by a culture that neglected safety, a bad barrel.

Founded in 1916, Boeing has been a leading US multinational company that manufactures airplanes. The airline industry is highly regulated, and recent investigations found that there were problems in the design of the aircraft and its systems, along with certification of the aircraft, in addition to problems of training and maintenance. Boeing admitted that the faulty automated system design was a factor in the 2018 and 2019 accidents.

The total cost to Boeing is not yet clear and will likely not be known for many years. Already, the financial cost is expected to be above $20 billion in lost revenue and compensation to customers and families. But it may be much higher. And that is in addition to the cost of human lives lost.

There were many stories of employees covering up deficiencies related to software and flight simulators and concealing problems from regulators. Some employees said that they would not want their families flying on the planes, and in 2017, before the crashes, one said that the "airplane is designed by clowns who are in turn supervised by monkeys."

US Congressman Peter DeFazio, leader of the House of Representatives investigation, said that the finding "paints a deeply disturbing picture of the lengths Boeing was apparently willing to go to in order to evade scrutiny from regulators, flight crews and the flying public even as its own employees were sounding alarms internally."

The CEO, Dennis Muilenburg, was fired after making overly optimistic predictions on how rapidly the problems could be fixed and pushing for approval from regulators. But his problems and the company's may have been more basic. There were messages in 2016 that the systems were faulty. And the company seemed to lack a culture that was focused on safety, which is critical to the business and industry. The design of the unsafe pilot software implicated in the crash may have been the work of a small group of employees, but their efforts were driven by a culture that rewarded them for design, and required pilot training (or certifying it was not needed) and disclosure (or lack of it), that valued efficiency and cost containment over safety.

This was clearly a bad barrel.

BP: Profit Pressure Leads to Deepwater Horizon Spill

In the mid-2000s, top management at BP, the global oil company, put pressure on its American subsidiaries to cut costs on refining operations and offshore drilling projects. The result was a series of preventable disasters that did lasting damage to the company and its reputation.

When the 2010 Deepwater Horizon drilling rig explosion in the Gulf of Mexico occurred, it became the largest environmental disaster in US history. The oil spill took eighty-seven days to control, caused eleven deaths, and led to enormous damage to the environment, onshore communities, and businesses, including commercial fisheries and tourism. The disaster eventually cost BP more than $65 billion, including over $18 billion in fines, the largest corporate settlement in US history. It caused the company to scale back several of its businesses and sell assets to pay the costs. This was a major disaster in every dimension.

Although not intentional, it was certainly negligent—and not an isolated incident for BP. In 2005, BP's Texas City, Texas, refinery exploded, killing fifteen employees and injuring about two hundred. It was the third fatal accident at the facility in four years, and BP admitted that safety procedures had been ignored. Between 1990 and 2004, BP had more accidents and spills than any other company in the country. In 2006, a poorly maintained pipeline leaked over two hundred thousand gallons of crude oil into Prudhoe Bay in Alaska, leading to both civil and criminal penalties. Also, as a result of numerous previous fines and violations at the facility, investigations found a series of prior related events and concerns over cost cutting and safety.

Although there have been numerous other serious incidents, the Texas City disaster and the Alaska spill certainly should have caused the company to revamp its systems and culture. Investigations after the 2010 disaster found safety violations that were similar to those found in the Texas City explosion. Specific recommendations for improvement at that time had not been implemented. There were reports, admissions, and commitments to change, but the violations at BP continued.

All this reflects a singular focus on profit and a lack of concern for legal requirements, worker safety, and social and environmental damage. In 2007, an independent review panel appointed by BP concluded that the company put profits before safety. Headed by former US secretary of state James A. Baker, the panel reported significant cultural failures at the company. A BP senior vice president concluded that the Texas City explosion had been "a preventable incident. It should be seen as a process failure, a cultural failure, and a management failure." Yet three years later, the same issues caused an even bigger disaster.

The Deepwater Horizon spill would have been costly to BP under any circumstances, but the fact that this was not an isolated incident makes it particularly dramatic. Sometimes unforeseeable events do happen, and that was BP's position. But although this may not have been intentional—in contrast to the Volkswagen case described earlier—it was certainly not surprising.

The deficiencies in governance, safety procedures, control systems, corporate culture, and ethics had made BP a crisis-prone organization. While the specifics of the

Deepwater Horizon disaster may not have been foreseeable, the likelihood of some type of disaster was.

In some instances of corporate misconduct, much of the blame falls on one or two leaders. At both BP and Boeing, a broad corporate culture focused on profits over safety, and there were systemic cultural failures throughout the organization. At BP in particular, leaders did not focus on serious issues even after lives were lost. If there had been a total overhaul of systems, ethics, and governance after the Texas City and Alaska disasters, Deepwater Horizon and its enormous costs in terms of damage to the environment, lost lives, and fines might never have happened.

HOW HAVE COMPANIES TRIED TO CREATE GOOD CULTURES?

As noted earlier, a good culture or reputation is built slowly over time, but it can be destroyed quickly by bad behavior. Many particularly strong ethical cultures have existed since the founding of companies. Hewlett-Packard's strong ethical culture of doing right by employees and customers lasted for fifty years, until both founders died. Marc Benioff's strong leadership of Salesforce since its founding has created and sustained an ethical and socially responsible culture. "This is just the way we do things around here," one Salesforce manager commented.

Even in founder-led companies, structures and communications strategies are needed to create and sustain an ethical corporate culture. In a company led by a professional manager, formal programs and repeated communication are the primary tools available. Over time, company efforts have settled on a common set of good practices. Most of these have been embodied in the US sentencing guidelines for judges and prosecutorial guidelines for federal prosecutors. The elements cited in these documents are standards, policies, and procedures; compliance program administration; communication, education, and training; monitoring and auditing; internal reporting systems; discipline for noncompliance; and investigation and remediation measures.

Over the past twenty years, corporate efforts have sought to implement these elements with a set of standard corporate practices. Companies, of course, vary widely in the skill with which they design these systems and efforts, and they vary even more widely in the seriousness with which they pursue them. As we will argue in chapter 5, many of these corporate programs are mere lip service, their effectiveness gutted by corporate indifference. Exhibit 3-1 lists twelve of the most common corporate practices, which we will explore more deeply in the sections that follow.

WRITTEN STATEMENTS

Companies generally adopt and publish statements describing their "corporate values" and their commitment to ethical behavior. These statements usually take two forms: a short statement of corporate values or a longer, more rule-oriented set of standards of business conduct.

Some companies simply adopt a few words to state the corporate values. Commonly used words include *innovative, profit driven, future oriented, disciplined, accountable,* and *integrity.* The word *integrity* requires definition and guidance on how it is to be traded off for other values, such as being "profit driven." Values statements should function as the foundation for describing ethical

EXHIBIT 3-1

CORPORATE PRACTICES TO CREATE
AN ETHICAL CULTURE

1. **Written statements**
2. Top-management **endorsement of ethics**
3. **Executive responsibility and adequate staff** for ethics programs
4. **Delegation of responsibility for ethics** to line managers
5. **Effective monitoring and auditing** of conduct
6. Enforcement of **standards and investigation** of and punishment for violations
7. **Training in ethics and compliance**
8. Creation of an **ethics hotline for reporting violations** and getting advice
9. Creation of a **no-retaliation** policy for those using the hotline
10. **Monitoring of the effectiveness** of the ethics program
11. **Regular oversight of the ethics program** by the board of directors
12. **Ethics risk assessments**

behavior in the corporation, but they usually fall far short of this objective.

Most companies' "standards of business conduct" describe, over many pages, the critical behavior standards they expect employees to follow, including not stealing company property, not revealing confidential information, not falsifying a financial or expense report, and not collaborating with competitors in ways prohibited by antitrust laws. More recently, such standards have included avoiding racial and sexual harassment and environmental violations, and protection of customer data.

Standards documents typically have several weaknesses. They primarily, and often exclusively, address standards that can be stated as clear bright-line rules, setting up the ability to discipline employees who violate them. They do not cover the hundreds of more subtle and nuanced behaviors that require balancing the interests among stakeholders or the application of a more general principle to a specific set of facts. This in turn gives the impression that the company is interested only in compliance, not action that reflects the more subtle values and value trade-offs.

Furthermore, standards typically address a generic set of concerns and are not informed by an analysis of specific areas of ethics risk for the particular company and the particular division or work group. In each case, there are areas of concern where employee misconduct is more likely and damaging. Codes rarely penetrate to the level where they would provide detailed guidance for employees in a specific function—engineering, sales, product design, and so forth. And of course, written values statements and business conduct guidelines depend entirely on how they are communicated to new and existing employees and whether they are perceived as lip service or genuine commitments.

TOP-MANAGEMENT ENDORSEMENT OF ETHICS

Virtually every company with a formal ethics program includes an endorsement, most often in print but sometimes as a video, from the chief executive about the company's values and standards of business conduct.

Such formal pronouncements rarely make an impact. For one, this may be the only time employees see the CEO's name associated with values other than profitability and growth. Moreover, many of the letters are so general, or so clearly written by others, that they are not taken seriously. In a few cases, the CEO's comments are actually counterproductive because his or her behavior is widely thought to be at odds with the company's values or standards of conduct. For example, Jeff Skilling and Kenneth Lay, the leaders of Enron, made formal statements in support of ethics, but in their day-to-day management of the company, they clearly operated differently.

There are obviously a few CEOs whose endorsement is credible and effective, but rare is the chief executive who gives unambiguous and consistent signals that ethics is a top priority when faced with business realities.

EXECUTIVE RESPONSIBILITY AND ADEQUATE STAFF FOR ETHICS PROGRAMS

No corporate initiative or standard is taken seriously unless there is a senior executive paying constant attention to it and adequate staffing to implement the programs that comprise it.

Sometimes a CEO will proclaim he or she is also the "chief ethics officer." Would that it were so! More commonly, supervision of ethics and ethics programs is assigned to an executive who has never had responsibility for profits and losses and is therefore not a good model for the balancing of ethics and business priorities. In many organizations, the executive assignment is given to the general counsel, whose primary responsibility is keeping the company out of trouble (or extracting it from trouble). If the general counsel has this role, it is too easy to see the ethics program as a legal and compliance exercise rather than a genuine attempt to put ethics to work in the company's decisions and operations.

DELEGATION OF RESPONSIBILITY FOR
ETHICS TO LINE MANAGEMENT

No initiative or objective in a corporation is taken seriously unless it is also a core responsibility of line management with profit-and-loss responsibility. However, it is a very rare company that has placed more than token accountability for ethics on line managers. More commonly, line managers have satisfied their ethical responsibilities if there is no major scandal in their operation.

While the ethics staff has grown and become more professional in recent years, too often it is seen as a powerless staff function or, worse, a naysayer to the legitimate pursuit of business and profit. Rare is the ethics executive who is respected for his or her business sophistication and past accomplishments. Even rarer is the ethics executive who moves on to senior executive responsibility. If employees know that there is a real investment in staff and programs to implement the ethics commitment, they are more likely to take it seriously.

EFFECTIVE MONITORING AND AUDITING OF CONDUCT

As in any area of corporate management, ethical and compliance behaviors must be monitored and audited to ensure they are followed and to signal that the company is serious about enforcing adherence to the proper behaviors.

Financial reporting is most commonly audited carefully, but recent scandals have shown that even those controls can be sidetracked. Sadly, chief auditors and chief financial officers have been culpable in some incidents of misconduct.

There is no chance, however, of motivating behavior and convincing employees that the company is serious about a standard of behavior if it is not tracked and measured. As we have seen in this chapter, safety efforts are particularly hard to measure, as is attention to ethical responsibilities beyond those to shareholders. Systems and controls are areas of great corporate emphasis and effort, but they remain weak in many areas of ethical concern.

ENFORCEMENT OF STANDARDS AND INVESTIGATION OF AND PUNISHMENT FOR VIOLATIONS

Once behaviors and standards are defined and adherence to them is audited and measured, no program would be successful without the enforcement of the desired behaviors, investigation of deviations, and punishment for those who violate the standards.

Many companies have ramped up their capacity for and skill in investigating violations of company standards. Encouraged by the US sentencing guidelines, which credit companies that themselves discover misconduct and investigate it, most large companies have created procedures to do this.

However, evidence suggests there are still disparities in how quickly violations by more senior executives or high performers are addressed and how seriously they are taken. Several companies have recently allowed senior executives accused of misconduct to retire rather than be fired and to vest their stock options and retirement plans when they do depart. For example, two executives credibly charged with sexual harassment were allowed to depart Google with a total of $135 million in exit packages in 2019.

Companies are making efforts to equalize punishments, but most admit they have not achieved this goal yet. There are very few cases where the board has stepped up and taken action for misconduct that might have been met with a slap on the wrist previously. The board of Hewlett-Packard fired the CEO, the late Mark

Hurd, for expensing the entertainment of a contractor with whom he was having a personal relationship. Ironically, he was immediately hired as co-CEO of Oracle and praised by Oracle's founder, who said HP's board should have overlooked the violation because Hurd was so talented.

TRAINING IN ETHICS AND COMPLIANCE

Any serious ethics program needs training efforts to educate employees regarding how to comply with the company values and standards. Most larger companies have introduced regular, usually annual, ethics training. In some areas of regulations and particular legal exposures, tailored training is offered to be certain that employees know the compliance expectations and to establish a basis for termination if an employee misbehaves. This is recently true in the area of sexual harassment—all employees are now typically trained annually or biannually on how to avoid misconduct.

Unfortunately, ethics training is of irregular quality in most organizations. In the best, well-prepared trainers backed up by local unit managers communicate the company's commitments to ethics and compliance and encourage discussion of how those commitments apply to the work of the local unit. When training takes place online, which it increasingly does, the opportunity to communicate strong local support and tailor the discussion to the work of a particular unit is reduced.

At its worst, ethics and compliance training is seen as an unreasonable burden and may be treated with derision. This can be due to poor training design or to the disinterest and disdain of the local managers and supervisors who order their organizations to undergo the training.

There is always pressure to reduce the substantial cost of training. In one case, a large multinational company required an annual half day of ethics training one year, a two-hour session the second year, a one-hour training the third year, then an online course, and finally training only if an employee failed a ten-question quiz on what some described as obvious ethical standards.

Training is not effective if it is not backed up by regular repetition and discussion. It is rare for a company to expect local managers to reinforce the ethics messages in periodic staff and management meetings or to apply them specifically to the work of the unit.

CREATION OF AN ETHICS HOTLINE FOR REPORTING VIOLATIONS AND GETTING ADVICE

Strongly encouraged by the US sentencing guidelines and other best-practices lists, most companies have created hotlines where employees can report misconduct by other employees or their bosses by phone, online, or in person. In recent years, these "whistleblowing" systems have become more sensitive, allowing employees to maintain anonymity. To encourage trust, many are now managed by outside organizations, creating another layer of anonymity to encourage trust in the system.

The availability of such a system is essential, but it is not the whole solution. A system that is easy to use and perceived as thorough and fair will encourage employees to uphold the standards themselves and to help flag misconduct by other employees. Before the last few years, however, ethics hotlines had mixed reputations. Reports are now being investigated more thoroughly, and those who report are being kept informed about the progress of investigations and the disposition of reports.

In recent years, some hotlines have been recast as "helplines," which also offer advice to employees who want assurance that they are doing the right thing in complex situations. Typically, though, the staff members who answer these inquiries are less effective at advising employees about ethics trade-offs than about bright-line compliance, and they often have limited understanding of the complex transactions that may be involved.

CREATION OF A NO-RETALIATION POLICY
FOR THOSE USING THE HOTLINE

Nothing is as important to the effectiveness of a hotline—or to encouraging employees to follow ethical commitments—than assuring them they will not suffer retaliation for raising an issue or reporting misconduct. Before hotlines, employees would rarely report misconduct by their bosses and even by peers. Supervisors could hurt their careers; peers could freeze them out of local teams.

Implementing a no-retaliation policy is difficult. Surveys still show that many employees, including a majority in some companies, fear using the hotline to report misconduct or even to ask a question. They are afraid that their bosses will learn of their anonymous report, and there are many ways retaliation can be hidden or blamed on poor performance.

When whistleblowers go public, or are forced to do so, their experience has been almost universally difficult. Their careers and reputations are typically badly damaged. The result is little confidence that no-retaliation policies really protect the ones who do the reporting.

MONITORING OF THE EFFECTIVENESS OF THE ETHICS PROGRAM

No program or culture remains strong without regular evaluation and improvement. While most companies understand that they must evaluate their ethics efforts, few have an effective method for doing so. Typically, companies use key performance indicators (KPIs) for ethics that focus on "input" factors, such as "100 percent of employees have taken ethics and compliance training," "the hotline functioned efficiently," and "investigations were launched and closed promptly."

These indicators give a very limited view of the true effectiveness of ethics efforts and the health of the ethical culture of the organization. What companies need is an evaluation of whether the ethics training is directed at both compliance and ethics and whether the training helps employees make the more complex and nuanced ethical choices that arise. Outcome measures are needed, such as an evaluation of whether the ethics program reduces misconduct or at least helps employees to know what to do when faced with ethical dilemmas.

It is a rare company that has a good measure of the health of its ethical culture—whether it is a good or bad barrel—and of which parts of the organization have the weakest cultures. A few consultants are now offering services purported to help companies measure the strength of the ethical culture, but these efforts are embryonic and vary greatly in quality. Most companies fall back on several questions typically asked in the periodic "employee climate" or "employee attitude" survey. Among these are questions like the following: "Do you trust your supervisor to follow the standards of business conduct?"

REGULAR OVERSIGHT OF THE ETHICS PROGRAM
BY THE BOARD OF DIRECTORS

The quality of the company's ethics program and the health of the ethical culture of the firm are strategic concerns appropriate for the board. Any genuine ethics commitment must have board endorsement and oversight.

Typically, however, ethics concerns are handled by boards through a committee, most often the audit committee, and consist only of a periodic report on investigations of misconduct and employee discipline. Ethics is rarely discussed by the full board of directors, except in the case of a major scandal. These procedures give the impression that the board is concerned only with compliance matters (investigations, discipline) focused largely on the past.

Some board committees, encouraged by revisions to the US sentencing guidelines, have tried to encourage the examination of "ethics risk." In this forward-thinking exercise, committees identify likely future violations and emerging issues.

ETHICS RISK ASSESSMENTS

The most recently recommended best practice among corporate ethics programs is the ethical risk assessment, undertaken either by the ethics and compliance group or by a risk-assessment unit elsewhere in the corporation. The US sentencing guidelines have encouraged risk assessment by rewarding companies that practice it when misconduct that results in federal conviction is punished.

To date, risk-assessment efforts are extraordinarily weak in most companies. If a company is highly regulated, it typically rates areas of compliance as ethically risky because the penalties can be so high. If a company has had a major scandal in the past, it will typically rate that area—financial reporting, product safety, sales practices, sexual harassment, or even a particular unit—as highly risky. But a more comprehensive and effective approach to ethics risk has been elusive and has had little impact on company operations or strategy.

To undertake an effective evaluation of ethics and compliance risk, both compliance standards and the company's own ethical values must be considered. Rarely have the company's ethical values been well codified or made explicit for the many functions of a corporation.

WHY MOST CORPORATE EFFORTS HAVE
FAILED TO PREVENT MISCONDUCT

We believe corporate efforts to date have failed to create and sustain ethical cultures. Bad barrels of various toxicity are still the norm.

The problem is not that most companies seek to act unethically but that they instead reduce ethics to compliance. Most companies still do not consider ethics and compliance to be a priority concern. The programs suffer from the perception that the purpose is not to get caught by regulators or prosecutors, and they therefore are regarded as little more than lip service. For far too many companies, implementing some form of the twelve practices described in this chapter has become a matter of compliance, of efforts to check the boxes, but not a genuine commitment to becoming a good barrel.

In 2019, the 189 CEOs of the Business Roundtable endorsed the principle that a company serves *all* its stakeholders, not just its shareholders. But the disconnect between these leaders' words and actions has created even more cynicism. Their companies have not sufficiently clarified both what that principle might mean in practice and what they are doing to implement that commitment. This fact is not lost on their own executives and employees who make their livelihoods in problematic corporate cultures.

Some companies speak clearly and credibly in ethics, but most do not. Ethics and compliance efforts remain a matter of lip service in many organizations. Very few companies truly know where their real ethics risks are and can design programs to audit those areas and clearly communicate what is expected of employees; the vast majority don't. Some boards take a genuine interest in their ethics programs; most go through the motions and nothing more.

Chapter 5 presents a program for corporations that want to take their ethical obligations seriously, describing how they can manage ethics in the organization and create good barrels for all to work in. But before we get there, we must turn our attention to the third possible source of continuing corporate misconduct: the competitive environments in which businesses operate. This is what we call the *bad-orchard problem.*

CHAPTER 4

The Bad Orchard: Some Competitive Environments Provoke Misconduct

Not all blame for corporate misconduct lies with bad apples or with bad barrels. A "bad orchard" is a competitive environment where ethical behavior is much more difficult, and misconduct is more likely.

Sometimes the setting is so difficult, we have some sympathy for executives and employees who misbehave. Local environments where bribery is common, for example, can make it hard to sell without bribing the purchasing officials. Situations where most firms ignore environmental regulations and gain a cost advantage can cut deeply into the profits of companies that follow environmental standards.

Consider the following cases of poisonous business environments that contributed to misconduct.

Airbus and Embraer: Bribery in the Aircraft Industry

Along with Boeing, European-based Airbus is one of the two biggest aerospace companies in the world. In 2020, Airbus agreed to pay the largest global settlement for bribery in history. The $4 billion fine, finalized with authorities in France, the United Kingdom, and the United States, was only half of what it otherwise would have been as a result of the company's cooperation in the investigation and its agreement to be subject to three years of monitoring.

The settlement ended fraud investigations into activities that covered the years from 2004 to 2016. Airbus was accused of using intermediaries to bribe public officials in numerous countries to buy its airplanes. Many illicit payments were made to hundreds of third-party agents in sixteen countries, including Japan, Russia, and China. Coded emails and fake names were used to hide the transactions. The bribery was pervasive and continued throughout its business for more than a decade.

Although the company paid the large fine, the settlement did not cover the individuals, including Airbus executives, who were involved; prosecutions are expected through the legal process, but that is likely to take years. Airbus fired over one hundred people for ethics and compliance violations as part of the investigations.

This is a case of serious corporate misconduct, but it was also not the first time for either the company or the industry. Airbus also had a previous major scandal in the 1990s, concerning payments made to officials of the Canadian government related to the purchase of Airbus jets by Air Canada.

There have been several other bribery and corruption cases in the aircraft industry, which demonstrates the prevalence of these issues in the industry and the challenges of operating in what is often seen as a bad orchard. Lockheed Corporation famously bribed Japanese members of Parliament and executives of Al Nippon Airline to buy its L-1011 in the 1970s, a case that led directly to the passage of the Foreign Corrupt Practices Act (FCPA).

In 2014, Brazil filed a criminal action against eight employees of Embraer, a Brazilian aircraft manufacturer, for paying a $1.5 million bribe to a Dominican Republic government official to obtain a $92 million contract. Millions of dollars of additional bribes were paid to other officials at airlines. Similarly, over $5 million was paid to secure a contract with the Indian Air Force.

The testimony and reports in this case, and related actions in the United States associated with government investigations, also suggested that the CEO, CFO, general counsel, and other senior executives of Embraer, the world's third-largest aircraft manufacturer (after Boeing and Airbus), were among those who knew and approved of the illegal payments. In 2016, the company paid over $200 million to the US government to resolve FCPA violations. Embraer admitted to bribing officials in Saudi Arabia, the Dominican Republic, and Mozambique.

A former Embraer vice president admitted that he engaged in a scheme to have Embraer pay bribes to a foreign official in exchange for an Embraer sales contract, retained a kickback as part of the scheme, laundered the proceeds through a South African company, and lied to law enforcement officials about his kickback. Embraer's operations in the bad orchard of the aircraft industry were compounded by its presence in Brazil, where corruption was peaking, highlighted by charges against a growing number of public officials and business leaders.

The competitive market of the major aircraft manufacturers is a clear example of a bad orchard. With only two to four manufacturers seeking mega-contracts for billions of dollars, sometimes decided by a few executives or government officials, there is a severe temptation to seek advantage through bribery or other means. Aircraft companies and their sales agents consider the bribes paid to individuals to influence their billion-dollar decisions as small change.

Equifax: A Breach of Customer Privacy

There are three major global consumer-credit-reporting agencies: Equifax, Experian, and TransUnion. Equifax aggregates information on more than eight hundred million consumers in addition to almost one hundred million businesses. It sells credit-monitoring data and other information directly to consumers and businesses.

In 2017, the personally identifying data of more than 145 million people were stolen from Equifax through a cybersecurity breach. In most cases, the stolen data included full names, Social Security numbers, birth dates, addresses, and driver's license numbers. In some cases, credit card information was also taken.

Equifax was widely criticized for numerous actions related to both the hack and the subsequent disclosures. First, investigators reported a lack of due diligence and protection of the data; there was substantial data vulnerability that should have been patched. The attackers were also able to retrieve data in encrypted form because of a lack of proper security processes.

To make matters worse, the company failed to publicize the breach until more than a month after it was discovered. In addition to the failure to disclose promptly to consumers and shareholders, this delay also gave executives time to sell their company stock, which led to charges of insider trading and the convictions of at least two executives.

As a result of the hack and the company's reaction to it, Equifax agreed to pay approximately $650 million to resolve lawsuits and investigations by state attorneys general, the Consumer Financial Protection Bureau, the Federal Trade Commission, and a consumer class-action lawsuit. The company also said that it spent more than a billion dollars on cleanup costs to improve data security.

When the breach occurred, the protection of the data, the response of Equifax leaders, and the disclosures to consumers were deemed inadequate and irresponsible. Hacking attempts and data breaches were becoming increasingly common, and Equifax had perhaps the most valuable set of data globally. The world of data had changed dramatically, becoming much more hostile, and Equifax had failed to respond.

With data privacy and due diligence central to the industry, changes in hacker behavior made the orchard more of a bad environment. Furthermore, broader concerns about privacy raised consumers' expectations. Before the breach, what was seen as a benign industry operating in a stable environment now appeared far more treacherous.

JPMorgan Chase: The Princelings of China

Doing business in China has long been an ethically risky proposition for Western companies. The dominant role of government in the economy, including the importance of "state-owned companies" in the economic and financial life of China, has created a minefield of difficulties for Chinese and Western companies alike. To secure business in China, companies often need to have the personal support of certain government officials or executives of state-owned companies. In a culture where relationships are most important in securing approvals, companies sought ways to do favors for these decision-makers.

In the early 2000s, JPMorgan Chase sought to expand its investment banking opportunities in the potentially lucrative Chinese market. Because many deals, particularly the largest, were subject to government influence, JPMorgan Chase's Asian executives sought to curry favor with key government officials. One method was to hire the sons and daughters of key officials for jobs with JPMorgan Chase. In a strategy known as the "Sons and Daughters Program," company officials tracked the hiring of so-called princelings on spreadsheets and openly discussed the financial gains from the hires. "How do you get the best quid pro quo from the relationship upon confirmation of the [job] offer?" asked one executive. Many, perhaps most, of the hired sons or daughters lacked the qualifications for their jobs. One son deemed "immature, irresponsible, and unreliable" was kept on for ten months after being derided in company emails. Chinese government officials were not shy about asking for jobs for an increasing number of "nephews" in addition to sons and daughters.

In 2013, the US Securities and Exchange Commission (SEC) initiated an investigation to determine if such practices violated the FCPA. In 2016, JPMorgan Chase agreed to a $264 million fine to settle the US investigation and promised to end the practice. JPMorgan Chase "engaged in a systematic bribery scheme by hiring the children of government officials and other favored referrals who were typically unqualified for the positions," said the director of the SEC Division of Enforcement. The agreement noted that the growth of JPMorgan's business in China had "an almost linear relationship" with the hiring program.

JPMorgan Chase also agreed to a three-year "nonprosecution" agreement to avoid criminal proceedings. The firm was required to implement an enhanced FCPA compliance program and to cooperate with government investigators. Other major investment banks, which had engaged in similar practices but to a lesser degree, also ended their "princeling" programs. Nonetheless, the need to build relationships in this bad orchard continued.

TYPES OF BAD ORCHARDS

We have found that bad orchards fall into one of the following five types, as summarized in exhibit 4-1:

Nations or Locales Where Most Companies Are Corrupt. First, a bad orchard could be an environment where some—or even the majority—of competitors are operating by different ethical rules. This could take the form of paying off customer representatives or government officials who buy the company's product or deliberately disobeying environmental or employment laws that are costly to follow. General corruption characterizes these bad orchards.

In this type of bad orchard, other companies may have a corrupt competitive advantage that is difficult to overcome. Their product is frequently bought not because it is better but because the competitor paid a bribe to a purchasing agent or a government official to block a competitor's access to the market. Both Airbus and JPMorgan Chase could argue that they operate in such an environment.

Industries or Locales Where Specific Bad Practices Are Common. Second, a bad orchard could be an industry or market where particular shortcuts have become common practice, such as the routine violation of one set of regulations. In some localities or industries, for example, there is widespread disregard for disposal regulations. In others, undisclosed ingredients are used that might be harmful to certain users. In still others, manufacturers are routinely sloppy about product safety or impacts on communities where raw materials are sourced. These highly specific misconduct practices may have grown up over a long time and are hard to change. Competitors have built the cost-saving practices

---

EXHIBIT 4-1

TYPES OF BAD ORCHARDS

1. **Nations or locales** where most companies are corrupt
2. **Industries** or locales where specific bad practices are common
3. Nations or locales where **corrupt governments** or organized crime dominate the economy
4. **Environment that "overreacts"** to bad news
5. **Capitalism** itself, according to some

---

into their business models, and regulators routinely look the other way, perhaps paid off with small gratuities or bribes.

Two cases of misconduct described earlier in this book, while primarily due to bad barrels or corporate cultures, are also due in part to this type of bad orchard. Volkswagen's defeat devices appear to mirror attempts by many automobile manufacturers to circumvent the testing procedures for pollution-control devices in other cars. Some observers argued that Volkswagen was simply doing what other European automobile manufacturers were doing, only more efficiently. Boeing's design of the flawed pilot software has some of the same characteristics. Boeing sought to hold down the operating costs of its airplanes by avoiding the requirement for retraining pilots. The airlines purchasing airplanes put significant pressure on the aircraft manufacturers to avoid these additional training costs.

The 1980s defense industry scandals, featuring $600 coffee-pots and fraudulent billing under government contracts, engulfed almost every large US defense contractor. Sloppy timekeeping and aggressive billing had become common practice in the industry and ensured that the companies were financially successful.

Nations or Locales Where Corrupt Governments or Organized Crime Dominate the Economy. Third, a bad orchard could be an environment where a powerful entity requires any firm operating there to conform to its norms, perhaps paying off certain officials for "protection" or hiring the children of officials. This is often an environment where the permission of an authoritarian government is required to do business or land a big contract.

Trash hauling in New York used to be regarded as this type of bad orchard because of the power of organized crime, which demanded payoffs and support of its other criminal ventures from any firm engaged in waste management. Fortunately, this specific bad orchard has been cleaned up significantly in recent years.

The corrupt power in these bad orchards may also be a particular political candidate or bureaucratic official. In some countries, market access can require permits and permissions granted only if the applicant supports the individual or party in power. In other cases, local officials whose routine permission is required to import goods or open a storefront can be representatives of the bad orchard.

This can even be true in the United States. In 1972, the reelection committee for President Nixon put great pressure on many large American companies to make illegal political contributions, threatening adverse regulatory decisions if they did not pay up. More than two hundred major corporations complied and were later convicted of campaign-funding violations.

Environment That "Overreacts" to Bad News. Fourth, a bad orchard could be an environment that excessively penalizes companies that miss their predicted quarterly earnings by even a penny. Where the market consistently "overreacts," some executives believe manipulation of financial results is justified. It could be an environment for corporate control, where failure to land a specific contract or to meet inflated goals would result in a shift of control to a rival faction or a wholesale replacement of management. It may be a market environment where any small safety or privacy violation is "blown out of proportion" by competitors or social media ready to exploit any weakness, causing the stock price to plummet. Executives may be too quick to blame this type of bad orchard for their misconduct, but such environments do exist.

When executives believe they operate in such an environment, the temptation is to cover up any small error or missed deadline, manipulate financial reports to meet quarterly expectations, and misrepresent technological or product development. Some companies found guilty of earnings "management" in the 2000s defended themselves by arguing they were protecting their firms from financial markets that "overreacted" to bad news.

Capitalism Itself, According to Some. Fifth, as discussed earlier, some consider the capitalist system itself a bad orchard. Critics argue that the profit motive ensures that every business will cheat and bribe at times. Misconduct, they argue, is endemic and inevitable in a capitalist system. This belief is behind the 1999 anti-globalization and anti–World Trade Organization riots in Seattle and the criticisms of business and the wealthy leveled by some Democratic candidates for president in 2020. The corporate scandals of the early twenty-first century, which engulfed almost all major financial institutions and a roster of the country's most prominent companies, have strengthened this critique.

These critics argue that the "invisible hand" of the free market, which is supposed to produce the common good from selfish behavior, actually encourages selfish behavior, inhumane decisions, and outright fraud. They believe that regardless of their personal values, religion, or understanding of the long-term consequences of unethical behavior, executives will choose short-term considerations to meet key goals or triggers for their own bonuses. Some critics contend that anyone who advocates anything less than a complete reform of capitalism, even the nationalization or control of corporations by government, is hopelessly naive.

The logic of self-interest is built into most corporate systems as well, corporate critics contend, tempting bad apples to seek personal enrichment and poisoning every corporate culture. Promotional systems reward the individual who meets his or her goals, regardless of how they are met. Performance evaluation emphasizes things that can be easily measured—sales volume, profit contribution, cost control—but not the social contribution a company makes or the goodwill in the community or in government. CEOs can reap huge bonuses by reducing investments in research and development (R&D) to increase short-term profits, although they know this will hurt the enterprise in the longer term. The pressures to meet performance goals can influence middle managers and lower-level employees as well.

Two trends in business seem to confirm the pressures executives face. One is the rapid turnover of senior executives whenever they miss a profit goal. Boards are driven by the market to replace executives for even short-term failure, thereby reinforcing the message to the whole organization that profit or share price is the top priority. The second trend is the increasingly active role of private equity and activist investors in corporate ownership and governance. Seeking to increase the value of their ownership stakes quickly, activist investors often force a shorter-term perspective on the firms they acquire.

Critics of capitalism point out that there is active opposition among many corporate executives and conservative economists to the whole notion of ethical business behavior. Ideologically driven, some executives believe that "free enterprise," dedicated exclusively to shareholder wealth, is the superior system and that any constraints on that behavior are dysfunctional for the society. Informed by the economic philosophy of Milton Friedman and others, many of these executives believe that it is an acceptable cost to have misconduct in business to harness free enterprise to produce wealth.

HOW DO BAD ORCHARDS DAMAGE
THE COMPANY AND SOCIETY?

Companies operating in bad orchards differ in their ability to avoid the pressures and temptations to conform to their environment.

Where widespread corruption exists, particularly bribery of public officials, companies secure contracts they are not qualified to perform and overcharge government buyers. A system of corruption in one area of government can infect other areas, and the bribes paid are often used not to improve society but to perpetuate rule by the corrupt group. Companies caught in this type of environment may cut corners on safety or produce substandard public works to save money and be competitive. The diversion of government funds to corruption can make it impossible for governments to invest in other priorities, such as roads, education, health, and public safety.

Corruption in the private sector causes no less damage. In several studies, the World Bank has argued that corruption impedes national economic development. Because bribes are being paid, the cost of goods is higher throughout the economy, and economic growth lags. Inside the individual company, corrupt actions beget other corrupt actions. Paying bribes to secure a few key sales seems, inevitably, to lead to paying bribes more broadly. Cheating on regulatory compliance leads to individual company units cheating in other venues—or even cheating the corporate headquarters or other divisions of the same firm. Entertaining customers in excess of company guidelines quickly spreads to expense-account cheating more broadly.

When some competitors ignore the firm's environmental and other impacts on society in order to keep their costs low, it is harder for other firms to address the legitimate concerns of all stakeholders. Companies get trapped in a "race for the bottom" as one or more firms in a market secure business by quoting low prices only possible through questionable practices. Poor behavior spreads virally throughout a market if one company "gets away with" the substandard behavior.

Consider the following case of the harm that can be done by a race-for-the-bottom industry.

Rana Plaza: Massive Deaths in the Garment Industry

On April 24, 2013, the catastrophic collapse of the eight-story Rana Plaza building on the outskirts of Dhaka, Bangladesh, killed more than 1,100 garment workers who were producing apparel for some of the world's largest retailers, including Gucci, Versace, Walmart, and many others. The building was designed to house stores and offices but was not considered structurally strong enough to support the heavy machinery needed in factories. The building's owners ignored warnings to close the building after cracks in the structure appeared the previous day.

The deadliest disaster in the history of the garment industry provides a new focus of corporate liability in terms of the safety of the global supply chain. Until the building collapsed, retailers used factory inspections and audits to claim their global supply chains were safe and in line with their business codes of conduct. But these inspections and audits were often grossly inadequate. In the wake of the disaster, there was an international push to hold companies accountable for the safety of buildings where their contractors have factories. Today, though, inspectors still find that very few companies have remedied their violations. Even those companies that are highly rated for labor and environmental performance seldom examine the safety standards for the buildings that their suppliers lease.

The Rana Plaza disaster reveals the challenge of a bad orchard. The garment industry has been pushed to compete on lower and lower prices, even at the expense of socially and ethically responsible environmental, labor, and safety practices. The retailers argue that they have little choice but to squeeze costs throughout the supply chain. The pattern is made worse because contracts to manufacture clothes are often for very short periods of time to meet an immediate fashion trend. This can lead to minimal oversight of production and an emphasis on cost alone. Historically, clothing manufacturing has shifted from country to country, seeking lower and lower costs—from the United States to China to Vietnam and now to Bangladesh. Many clothing companies contracting for the clothes to be made refuse to look carefully at the dangerous and poor working conditions throughout their supply chains. However, for some companies, the disaster at Rana Plaza has caused a new examination of the extent of their legal, social, and ethical responsibilities and liabilities.

ARE BAD ORCHARDS MORE OF A PROBLEM TODAY?

Bad orchards have always been a feature of the market system. Market environments are never perfectly competitive, and successfully negotiating those imperfect environments is critical for ethical operation.

To some critics, capitalism creates a "race to the bottom." Those who question the morality of the system argue that it drives one or more competitors to cut prices, trim any socially useful behavior, and then cut legal or regulatory corners in order to quote even lower prices. This tendency robs a community and society of important investments in social and environmental goals and tends to corrupt the community and broader society as corner-cutting becomes the norm. The ethical firm, these critics argue, will never compete successfully.

With the globalization of business in the twenty-first century, there are more opportunities for companies that operate by lower environmental or human rights standards to take business from more responsible companies. Global companies operate in some countries or markets where the business standards are lower than, or different from, those in the developed world. Dealing with corruption in Asia, Africa, or Latin America is an unavoidable task of any successful global enterprise.

Many executives argue that the stock market today is less tolerant of any small misstep in quarterly sales or earnings. "Short-termism," they argue, makes it impossible for a chief executive to pay attention to anything beyond the narrow financial interests of the shareholder and gives great incentives to manipulate earnings and cover up missteps. This has been heightened further in recent years by a growing cadre of corporate "raiders" or "activist shareholders," which has increased the pressure on corporate leaders to keep performance steady, no matter the cost. CEOs, who value their jobs more highly because of greatly increased compensation, are tempted to cut corners to "make the numbers." Long-term investment—in R&D as well as ethics programs and social responsibility activities—is more difficult than ever.

While global anti-corruption campaigns have cleaned up some corrupt environments, the rise of more authoritarian states and leaders in the twenty-first century has created new pressures. Many American companies have struggled with increasing demands from autocrats, as well as ethical questions about whether to collaborate or resist the policies of national and foreign leaders. Some leaders have threatened retaliation against individuals and companies that don't comply with requests or publicly disagree with their policy initiatives.

Some who track the changing capitalist system argue that all these forces have increased the intensity of competition and made doing successful ethical business in a capitalist system that much harder.

HOW HAVE COMPANIES TRIED TO
MANAGE BAD ORCHARDS?

Companies have tried a variety of strategies to compete effectively in difficult environments, to insulate themselves from those bad orchards, and in some cases, to change those environments for the benefit of everyone.

We have identified at least five generic strategies employed by companies to cope with bad orchards, as summarized in exhibit 4-2:

Vigorous Competition on Quality, Service, and Price. Some companies simply seek to outcompete the companies engaging in substandard behavior. By offering products and services that are significantly higher quality, they seek to make it harder for buyers to purchase others' inferior products and services. By running a leaner and more efficient business, they hope to reduce their own costs enough to quote significantly lower prices. And they take in stride the loss of some contracts they should have won.

Avoidance. A second strategy is avoidance. Companies have made the difficult decision not to start doing business in, or to exit from, a country or industry that is a bad orchard. This action is not taken lightly and usually follows an extensive internal debate. In some cases, executives have concluded that trying to operate ethically in certain bad orchards will simply never be profitable or will inevitably lead to scandals that the company wants to avoid.

Constructive Engagement, Often with Collective Action. A third strategy is constructive engagement, which involves working with and through industry associations and proper authorities to try to make the environment less of a bad orchard. This third strategy is often accompanied by *collective action*, creating an industry-wide or economy-wide voluntary campaign and commitment to stopping corruption or the offending practice. Many firms have

---

EXHIBIT 4-2

GENERIC STRATEGIES FOR COPING
WITH BAD ORCHARDS

1. **Vigorous competition** on quality, service, and price
2. **Avoidance**
3. **Constructive engagement**, often with collective action
4. **Enlisting the power of government**
5. **Adopting a "follow local practices" strategy**

---

joined Transparency International chapters in countries with patterns of corruption, working to build coalitions of companies that will eschew bribery or put pressure on government to do more to fight the corruption.

Enlisting the Power of Government. A fourth strategy is enlisting the power of government by sponsoring new laws and regulations meant to control the behavior of bad actors. This can level the playing field for all companies if government is willing, if the laws are well written, and if they are fairly enforced. Of course, there are some cases where businesses have used government action and regulation to give a particular firm or industry an advantage, thereby creating a bad orchard for others. But some companies have deliberately partnered with prosecutors to conduct investigations of their own industries to uncover the widespread misconduct of competitors.

Adopting a "Follow Local Practices" Strategy. The fifth strategy is to follow the standards of the bad orchard. There are obviously many firms that choose to operate by the corrupt standards of their competitors. Some executives, when pressed to explain this behavior, argue that they have no choice but to follow the standards of the local market. They will sometimes embellish this argument with the claim that they have no right to impose their values on local governments or markets. "It would be economic imperialism to impose our anti-corruption values on other societies," argued one executive we know. At other times, the executives argue that "going along with the crowd" is simply leveling the playing field and giving themselves a "fair" chance.

Companies have sometimes been aided in coping with bad orchards abroad by US laws and regulations, as well as some state and local laws aimed at prohibiting and penalizing overseas misconduct. The best known of these is the FCPA, passed in 1978 in the wake of the discovery that hundreds of blue-chip US companies were paying bribes abroad. The FCPA makes it illegal for any company doing business in the United States to bribe government officials abroad. The *extraterritorial* application of this law reinforces incentives for US companies operating in the United States to conduct themselves ethically in bad orchards abroad. It can also pressure foreign companies to operate ethically abroad if they also want to do business in the United States.

It is not just the United States that has passed laws with extraterritorial impact. The UK's Bribery Act of 2010 and the European Union's General Data Protection Regulation (GDPR) apply to almost every large company in the world.

The effectiveness of these many strategies in reducing the company's own misconduct in bad orchards varies widely. Some companies have such a competitive advantage, built on defensible intellectual property or other factors, that they can successfully outcompete others that would engage in corrupt practices. Nonetheless, they pay a price to operate in these difficult environments in terms of lost business and higher costs to police their own organizations. Individual employees will always be tempted by the chance to win a sale that might be lost to a competitor willing to pay off a buyer.

More common are companies that claim to operate entirely free of corruption but whose enforcement of that standard with its own employees is weak. Some organizations creatively search for alternatives to outright corrupt payments. One particular company that had been banned from bribing foreign officials found opportunities to sponsor "inspection trips" for foreign buyers, which included extended family vacations at Disney World and generous per diem arrangements. In other instances, as noted in the JPMorgan Chase case, the children of officials and buyers had been given jobs or awarded "scholarships" to attend US universities by the companies seeking to sell their products and services. Enforcement by federal prosecutors struggles to catch up with these work-arounds.

Engagement strategies have been effective in some cases, particularly where local government and the local business community have been seeking allies to promote more vigorous enforcement of anti-corruption laws. With the recent rise of more autocratic governments, however, many engagement efforts have been unsuccessful. Some bad orchards are getting worse.

Companies have generally been unwilling to promote the adoption of new laws and regulations to control the behavior of less ethical companies. High-tech companies, for example, are hesitant to accept new laws designed to rein in some of the outlaws of the internet, fearing that whatever standards were written would be overly restrictive and impossible to implement, and might put them at a disadvantage.

Companies have had limited success in disrupting entrenched advantages given by governments to specific companies or industries. Uber, the ride-hailing company, has argued that local rules in many, if not most, cities and states have favored legacy taxi companies, requiring superfluous licensing and permits to operate or pick up and drop off at airports. As a result, Uber developed a strategy of deliberately disobeying some of these regulations, forcing public officials to change them or look the other way. This kind of strategy can demonstrate a disregard for the law and for ethics in general, an attitude that has arguably influenced the corporate culture of Uber. Frequently, companies that might have brought innovations into a particular market have decided, instead, to stay out.

Companies have tried various strategies to cope with the demands of the financial market for short-term results, without significant success. Executives talk more articulately about long-term investments and strategies; some no longer give quarterly and annual "advice" about expected earnings. Nonetheless, analysts still watch quarterly earnings closely.

Among the most troublesome of the financial pressures of bad orchards is that of activist investors who buy blocks of company stock in order to demand higher short-term earnings and build pressure on the current leadership of the company. Such activities seek to "unlock" shareholder value by restructuring companies and adopting new strategies, sometimes geared to cutting costs dramatically. Activists are criticized for creating bad orchards by making longer-term investments in R&D, environmental and energy transformations, and employee retraining impossible. Companies are relatively unsuccessful in resisting the pressure of activist investors.

Recently, a few executives and leading companies have tried to convince others that capitalism is not such a bad orchard and that businesses can operate by ethical standards. The 2019 Business

Roundtable statement on corporate responsibility and the 2020 Davos Manifesto are examples of leadership efforts to demonstrate that companies are dedicated to all their stakeholders and to nudge reluctant corporations to do so. UN Secretary-General Kofi Annan, who held that office from 1997 to 2006, launched the UN Global Compact in 1999 to urge companies to commit to ten principles of ethical behavior, but critics have argued that it has had little effect on real corporate behavior. Too often, these statements do not represent the actual beliefs and practices of most of the world's companies but are adopted for public relations purposes.

One reform-minded group has sought to change the *legal* structure of capitalism to make it a better orchard. The benefit-corporation or B-Corp movement promotes the reincorporation of businesses as public-benefit entities, which have social benefits as well as profits as *explicit* corporate objectives. Enabling legislation in more than thirty-five states adopted during the 2010–20 period allows a corporation to register itself as a B Corp. Such a step can permit a company to attract talent that might not choose to work for a company with a narrower set of objectives and can help protect the company from activist shareholders who seek to replace management because financial returns are lower while pursuing social goals. The firms that register in this way work with a supporting organization called B Lab, which helps the companies honor their dual purposes. The advocates of this movement hope to demonstrate that having a broader mission can be as profitable as serving shareholders alone. To date, however, few large or medium-size companies have incorporated or reincorporated as B Corps.

THE ROLE OF BAD ORCHARDS

Bad orchards exist and explain a substantial amount of corporate misconduct and scandal. Companies choose to operate by the standards of those bad orchards or succumb to the temptations and incentives there. As noted earlier, some executives and companies exploit the bad-orchard argument, contending that misconduct should be forgiven because they were just trying to "level the playing field." This argument is unacceptable.

In one of our executive business school classes a few years ago, an American executive argued that bribery was essential for his firm to operate successfully in a Latin American country because "everyone there bribes." Two executives from that country who were also in attendance grew increasingly angry and confronted him publicly in class, arguing that there was a robust anti-corruption effort in the country and a growing percentage of companies that refused to pay bribes. "Your company is holding up efforts to fight corruption in our economy," they told the American executive. "Join us."

In a well-publicized case, Walmart found that the executives in its Mexican subsidiary were bribing local officials to get approvals to open new stores. This behavior was not an attempt to "level the playing field" but an attempt to tip it in favor of Walmart by winning the right to open their stores first.

Managing in bad orchards is a critical skill of any management team. Corporate executives need to be creative enough to find ways of getting things done in difficult competitive environments without violating ethical norms. We acknowledge, however, that there are bad orchards where profitable ethical business is impossible. In those cases, management must have the courage to look elsewhere for business opportunities.

CHAPTER 5

Decisive Actions Companies Must Take to Improve Ethical Performance

We have been critical of current corporate efforts to manage ethical behavior. Companies have created substantial organizations and strategies to address ethics and compliance, but these endeavors haven't been enough to curb misconduct. What more should they be doing?

We believe that companies need a fundamentally new understanding of the challenge they face and a greatly enhanced level of commitment. Efforts to date, extensive as they have been, have fallen far short of what is needed to create and sustain an ethical corporation in the twenty-first century. Without a major rethinking of what is needed, eye-opening corporate scandals will continue, and the human and economic damage done will increase.

The already-shaky support for the free-market system will be further eroded.

There is a particular challenge to address corporate misconduct in a post-COVID-19 era. On the one hand, companies are weaker economically and may face greater pressure for short-term earnings. On the other hand, so many of the conventional assumptions about how companies operate have been disrupted that they may have a chance to write a different story. It is also possible the public will demand more responsible corporate conduct, having witnessed both good and egregiously bad corporate behavior during the pandemic.

There will always be pressures and incentives on corporate leaders to act in ways that favor short-term profits over long-run sustainability. And there will always be the temptation to commit minor violations that put a company or an individual on a slippery slope that leads to more serious misconduct. While some executives and employees will be able to resist the pressure to misbehave, others will compromise their standards at the slightest hint of pressure or potential embarrassment. Some will adopt clear ethical principles for their organizations, and others will reduce ethics to compliance, even blaming their own misconduct on poorly written laws and regulations.

This chapter describes ten strategies that executives, boards, and companies need to adopt if they are to have a chance of creating and sustaining an ethical organization, one that is less likely to experience misconduct in the future. Some of these strategies involve new practices, but others address how companies need to strengthen existing practices.

These ten strategies embody a new approach that places social purpose, values, and ethics at the core of the organization;

establishes leaders as moral exemplars; and goes far beyond what has been done before. Our recommendations are as follows:

1. Define a new approach to corporate purpose.
2. Create purpose-driven business strategies.
3. Set a new tone at the top through genuine moral leadership.
4. Enhance line accountability for purpose and ethics.
5. Expand the portfolio of the ethics and compliance officer to include "macro-ethics."
6. Establish a transparent and safe environment for communication about ethics.
7. Routinely evaluate incentives and systems based on core values.
8. Implement new techniques to anticipate ethical impacts and risks.
9. Increase board accountability for corporate purpose and ethical behavior.
10. Reform existing ethics and compliance programs.

Companies may be quick to say they are already doing all these things. We know. We have worked with dozens of leading companies around the world, and although they think they are doing them, they most often are not—or at least are not doing them well. Most corporate efforts have been limited to the standard ethics and compliance practices. They have also frequently been badly designed and implemented in a half-hearted way. We are calling for a new approach, involving leadership commitment among top executives and boards that has never existed before.

All ten initiatives are essential for an effective organization that simultaneously reduces ethical risk and improves both ethical and financial performance.

DEFINE A NEW APPROACH TO CORPORATE PURPOSE

What does a new definition of corporate purpose mean in practice? The 2019 publication of the "Business Roundtable Statement on Corporate Responsibility" laid bare the central weakness of corporate ethics efforts. A very general and ambiguous commitment to take the interests of all stakeholders into account allows companies to continue to operate as usual. It does not require any new actions; companies can always find a few examples of how business decisions and practices motivated solely by profit or reputation served another stakeholder in addition to shareholders.

The new definition of corporate purpose must be different from, and stated differently than, what companies espouse today. Companies must explicitly state the social purpose and social usefulness of the company's products and services. Stating this purpose in this way will establish strong guidelines for the design of products and services, as well as how they will be marketed and delivered. The company's other purposes—to provide an adequate return to the providers of capital, the shareholders; to provide adequate compensation to employees; and to create mutually beneficial relationships with business partners and communities—should all facilitate the core social purpose.

Companies often embrace a social purpose in times of natural disasters and emergencies. In the wake of hurricanes and tornadoes, some companies act quickly to meet local needs in fulfillment of a core purpose to put corporate capabilities to work for the community. In the early days of the COVID-19 crisis, some companies rushed aid to health-care systems lacking protective gear. Stating a clear commitment to this type of social action could be part of the company's newly articulated "purpose."

The stated social purpose must be accompanied by a broader commitment to integrity and ethical operation, which goes beyond the law. An example might be: "The company will never violate the law nor ethical principles of fair treatment of all its stakeholders. The company will not mislead customers nor misrepresent its products or services. The company will never hide features of its products that affect the interests of its customers."

Corporations are quick to invoke a very general commitment to ethics but very hesitant to describe in detail what that means. "Do no evil" or "Always act with integrity" are anemic statements of ethical commitment, as is "Always comply with the law." These statements give little real guidance to the organization's members on how they are to act. Stating the company's guiding ethical principles strongly and in enough detail will establish specific ethical guideposts for executives and staff that are typically missing in today's organizations.

The importance of stating a company's social purpose has been evident during the COVID-19 pandemic. Many publicly traded companies were first in line for CARES Act benefits and exhausted the funds available before most small firms could qualify. In doing so, they were simply operating by conventional logic and an exclusive financial purpose. If it is legal, then management should take advantage of the forgivable loans to reduce losses. Some firms did ultimately give back their CARES funds, but a cynic may conclude that they simply succumbed to public pressure. If a company were committed to a purpose that included a community role and a commitment to help in times of disaster, such a firm might have behaved differently.

A minimalist approach to purpose, ethics, and compliance is not enough. Only an explicit, specific, and credible commitment to social purpose, to the welfare of all stakeholders—not just to shareholders—will be enough.

CREATE PURPOSE-DRIVEN BUSINESS STRATEGIES

After adopting a clearly defined corporate purpose that is well communicated, a company must develop and assess business strategies that clearly and explicitly align with that purpose and its ethical commitments.

Few companies have taken this step of connecting strategy explicitly to corporate social purpose by creating internal systems and procedures to make it happen. Typically, corporate strategic assessments and announcements emphasize only how a new product or other strategic step will enhance growth and profitability. Employees in the firm are reminded by this repetition—and the omission of any other criterion—that these are the only purposes of the company.

Stock buybacks in the 2017–19 period were a popular corporate strategy and were designed to increase the stock price rather than develop more socially useful products or services, research climate-friendly processes to mitigate climate change, prepare for major disruptions such as the pandemic, or bolster the company's financial strength to meet future needs. Private equity companies, which took hundreds of nursing homes private in the 2010s, sold off their real estate, creating great wealth for their owners but leaving nursing homes thinly staffed and wholly unprepared for the COVID-19 pandemic.

All proposed business strategies must be evaluated formally on their capacity to further the company's purposes and their consistency with the company's ethical commitments. They must identify the risks that may frustrate the company's stated social purpose or violate the rights or interests of one or more stakeholders. Reducing investment in safety at BP had those risks prior to the Deepwater Horizon spill, but they were apparently disregarded; ramping up the pressure on the sales force created those risks at Wells Fargo, but management considered them acceptable even as hundreds and thousands of employees engaged in blatant misconduct. There is no evidence that either company discussed these possibilities and the potential impact on long-term profitability when the strategies were being considered.

One of the strongest dynamics in business is the search for new products and new services to sell to new markets. Each proposed research or product-development project should be analyzed for its alignment with the social purpose of the company. So should new sources of supplies and new financing arrangements. Companies take significant risks if their sales organizations will cut corners and do whatever it takes to close deals and if their operating organizations will ship products without adequate testing or safety checks in order to meet quarterly financial goals. A process for examining every strategy and significant decision through the lens of purpose and ethical responsibility will moderate those risks.

Every company needs a formal process for the assessment of new business initiatives and strategies if alignment is to be achieved. The overwhelming dominance of shareholder interest and short-term profitability leads to inevitable compromises in serving other stakeholders. Only formal systems and procedures can weigh against this.

SET A NEW TONE AT THE TOP THROUGH
GENUINE MORAL LEADERSHIP

Striking the right "tone at the top" has become a mantra for corporate ethical leadership in recent years. Most corporate leaders are confident that they have strongly communicated their desire for integrity in the organization and have set a good example for their employees. Sadly, most have not done enough and are not seen as the moral leaders they imagine themselves to be.

CEO speeches and statements on values and ethics are often so general that they are seen as lip service, and they often *are* lip service. In a large number of companies, the predominant view is that management is focused only on following the letter of the law or even on not getting caught. After the Wells Fargo crisis was disclosed, the CEO said that "the culture of the company is strong and based on ethics and doing what's right," which led members of the US Congress to suggest he was "tone-deaf and in denial."

A new approach to corporate leadership and communication, a new tone at the top, is needed. Employees take their cues from what is talked about day to day in the organization. The company that is obsessed with growth and profit margins, and incidentally states that it wants integrity, is vulnerable to misconduct. A CEO who speaks about ethics only in the annual reissue of the code of conduct is not a moral leader.

This new type of moral leadership requires a constant focus on the social and moral purpose of business, as well as on what ethics and integrity mean specifically for the company. CEOs must be known personally for their integrity and ethical courage. Boards need to consider whether candidates for CEO are considered moral leaders. Most often, boards simply ask if there are any "ethical problems" in a candidate's background, not whether he or she is good at moral leadership. Moral leadership should be a formal requirement for promotion to senior management.

Corporate leaders cannot rely on assigning internal communication to a communications department or to an ethics organization. It requires a relentless and daily communication from the CEO and other top officers of the company's purpose and ethical commitments. The leader needs to share frequently, for example, how new strategies fulfill and are aligned with the company's purpose and ethical commitments. In this way, the effective moral leader must be a storyteller who describes how past and present decisions reflect the company at its best.

Moral leaders must also be willing to label bad behavior for what it is. This requires them to talk about where their own company has failed to act in an acceptable manner. It also involves calling out unethical behavior by competitors or others in the company's environment. Most executives go silent in the wake of misconduct by others, justifying their silence as "not wanting to hit a man when he is down." This leaves the impression that the behavior is acceptable, that the company may have done the same thing but just did not get caught.

ENHANCE LINE ACCOUNTABILITY FOR PURPOSE AND ETHICS

Not much has been expected of line executives and midlevel managers in ensuring that a company operates ethically. This must change.

Typically, the line manager is only asked if his or her organization has completed the required corporate ethics and compliance training. The manager may also be required to speak once a year to the organization about ethics, but little else. The executive or manager will only be penalized if the division or unit has a major scandal or a consistent pattern of violations or hotline reports.

Real shared accountability for the purpose and ethics of the corporation requires much more. First, it must include a detailed and thoughtful interpretation of the purpose and ethical commitments of the company to the work of the specific division or unit. If there is a commitment to products or services that serve a particular social purpose, then the manager in charge of every unit must spend the time to state clearly for that unit's employees how their specific work fulfills the purpose and commitment to integrity. The manager must institute the systems and procedures to evaluate whether proposed strategies, policies, products, and services further the purpose and fulfill the company's commitment to ethics.

There are hundreds of opportunities in the course of a year for a manager to comment on existing or new strategies or decisions, relating them to purpose and ethical commitments as well as growth and profitability. But getting the tone right is not an easy task. Explaining how each new product "improves lives around the world" or fulfills an ethical commitment can be difficult. Nonetheless, this kind of communication will enable the line or middle manager to set a moral tone for the division or unit and give explicit guidance on how the balance between profit and ethics is to be achieved.

EXPAND THE PORTFOLIO OF THE ETHICS AND COMPLIANCE OFFICER TO INCLUDE "MACRO-ETHICS"

It is a rare corporate ethics and compliance officer who is asked, or permitted, to play a role in assessing the ethics of major corporate decisions or strategies. Instead, the chief ethics and compliance officer (CECO) and his or her staff members are usually charged with ensuring that compliance standards are communicated effectively to a company's employees and that hotline reports are investigated and resolved. One corporate ethics officer has called this a "micro-ethics" approach.

Ethics and compliance staffs are generally considered to be doing a good job if senior management can be confident that the company will not be criticized publicly for a lack of compliance effort. The ethics and compliance staff must be seen to address reports of misconduct promptly, investigating all cases and imposing whatever remedies are called for. The more empowered staff members follow up with recommendations for changes in systems and procedures throughout the company, but such recommendations too often go unheeded.

"Macro-ethics" issues are the ethical dimensions of the major and minor strategic decisions the company makes—such as those regarding new products and markets, new financing instruments, and mergers and acquisitions. These decisions most often have significant ethics implications or risks and need to be implemented in a manner consistent with the company's ethical principles. Yet often, there is no one at the table whose role is to raise those issues or suggest how to implement the decisions in ethical ways.

Occasionally, a confident CEO, or a board, will appoint a corporate officer or designate a member to ask questions and express opinions regarding the ethics of major decisions. This should become a standard practice, although its effectiveness will still depend on whether the CEO and senior management group, or the board members, listen to the counsel given and take it seriously. The success of this role will also depend on how knowledgeable the individual is about the business of the company and its finances, as well as the company's purpose and ethical commitments.

Ethics should be at the table whenever a major initiative is being considered.

ESTABLISH A TRANSPARENT AND SAFE ENVIRONMENT FOR COMMUNICATION ABOUT ETHICS

One of the most significant characteristics of a healthy ethical culture is that employees feel empowered and safe enough to participate with their managers in achieving the company's purpose and upholding its ethical commitments. Company leaders must create an open and safe culture where employees can raise unresolved questions about the application of the purpose and goals to their own work and about directives given to them by the supervisors and managers in their chain of command. They need to be empowered to live the values of the company day to day and pursue the stated corporate purpose.

This is one of the most challenging tasks management has in most companies. Often, employees feel intimidated by the power of those who can affect their opportunities, the conditions of their employment, and even their continued employment. They may have concerns about a questionable directive they receive, but in the end they feel compelled to suppress their ethical qualms for fear of angering their bosses or even losing their jobs. Company non-retaliation policies are often of limited credibility to employees, who know there are many subtle ways to retaliate against the employee who raises a difficult ethical question. Employees are also aware of the sorry stories of whistleblowers in business and government who have suffered unjustly for raising legitimate questions.

To overcome these barriers, companies must go further than they have to create an open and transparent culture. Companies must take the initiative to ask what challenges employees face in living out the company's commitments frequently, rather than waiting for them to raise such issues. Employees will often know the actual impact of policies and programs on different stakeholders better than their bosses. But employees will never share their insights unless they are asked and unless they trust management to use this information responsibly.

Ethics can only be managed effectively in any organization by an active dialogue between the senior management and all employees. There should be a continuous process, through surveys and other means, to allow employees to give advice on how the company can achieve its goals and align its ethical commitments more effectively. This dialogue needs to take place through periodic in-person discussions of the ethics of the work of each unit.

A candid dialogue also requires a process to push contrary opinions up in the organization so that opposing views are heard by senior management. In many corporate ethics scandals in recent years, a sizable group of employees knew of the violations or knew of serious culture issues but said nothing. Employees told investigators that they did not know whom they could tell or who would listen. They doubted their own supervisors would be interested because they never talked about ethics. Others said they simply did not trust senior management to address the issue.

Companies no longer have any alternative to such openness and transparency. In the era of social media, employees will express their collective voice, whether the company facilitates it or not.

ROUTINELY EVALUATE INCENTIVES AND
SYSTEMS BASED ON CORE VALUES

Corporate purpose and ethical commitments are embodied in innumerable formal and informal systems, particularly those related to incentives. Corporate leaders should ensure that every incentive program, every system, and every routine in the company contributes to achieving its purpose and its ethical commitments.

Setting goals and the incentives to achieve them is a nuanced process. Goals have to be challenging, but not so challenging that they encourage unethical behavior or inadvertently signal that employees are to meet the economic goals at any cost. The design of systems and processes has the same risk: it may facilitate or frustrate the achievement of purpose and ethical behavior. Every system must be examined for how it can be "gamed" by the employee who would abuse it.

The goals, incentive regimes, and all types of systems need to be constantly scrutinized to ensure that they contribute to the accomplishment of the corporate purpose, ethical commitments, and compliance. Periodic reviews of all systems are important, but a standard procedure should be put in place that reviews all new programs and procedures for their ability to motivate the right kind of behavior—and their resistance to motivating the wrong kind of behavior.

Informal incentives must also be addressed. Challenging orthodoxy in organizations, for example, is occasionally an informal norm and is applauded. Pushing boundaries, being creative, and "thinking out of the box" can, at times, produce great corporate results. But informal values and incentives such as these need to be monitored very carefully. Enron, for example, was widely praised for years for its out-of-the-box financial thinking, which eventually led to fraud and the largest bankruptcy in US history.

Goals, incentives, and systems are interpreted within the broader informal culture of each company. Some companies have a "no excuses" culture where goals are to be met at any cost, even if corners have to be cut or procedures violated. Individual middle managers within the same organization can establish different expectations. Some managers give a clear indication of their attitude of "don't tell me how you met the goal; just meet it." Other cultures are more forgiving or more committed to meeting the spirit and the letter of compliance standards or the company's own ethical commitments.

Failure to assess incentive programs and systems can be disastrous. It is clear no one questioned the sales incentives at Wells Fargo, for example. Some of the other major ethical disasters in recent years, such as Volkswagen and BP, also featured poorly designed goals and incentive systems.

Management needs to acknowledge that performance measures and systems can indeed motivate people to act in ethical or unethical ways. It is essential that every incentive program and system be formally evaluated for its ethical content. The more "stretch" the goals are, the more some employees will justify to themselves that the company wants them to cut corners and violate procedures.

More complex systems and incentives have been introduced in many organizations. This requires new analytic skills, and maybe even a new profession of systems designers and evaluators, to design and audit these systems for their real impact. It is critical to consider in detail the ways that some employees might attempt to beat the systems. New insights from the evolving field of behavioral ethics can inform this process.

IMPLEMENT NEW TECHNIQUES TO ANTICIPATE
ETHICS IMPACTS AND RISKS

The achievement of social purpose and the management of ethical behavior in the corporation require a new approach to ethics risk analysis.

Formal ethics scanning should be adopted to evaluate all proposed products, services, policies, and marketing campaigns. Every one of these presents a unique set of opportunities and risks—opportunities to enhance the accomplishment of both corporate social purpose and economic goals and risks that they may frustrate the achievement of social purpose or violate important ethical principles in the name of economic growth.

Scanning is also critical to examine the likely effects of new technologies. Companies are increasingly being required to take responsibility for their own technical infrastructures—for example, new platforms, techniques for data collection and storage, surveillance, genetic testing, and protection and privacy of data. There is an obligation to flag problems early and participate in the solution. When companies fail to scan—or fail to act on what they learn—there are often ethical, legal, and financial responsibilities.

Upon the adoption of formal ethics scanning and analysis, all existing products, services, policies, programs, and systems should be examined using the same process. This retrospective analysis may uncover lurking ethics risks the company has not identified. Changes in the social, political, and economic environment create new ethical risks, along with increased business risks, so a second type of scanning would examine external changes that may create new ethical risks to the company or new opportunities for the accomplishment of the corporation's social purpose as well as its economic goals. The #MeToo and Black Lives Matter movements created both new risks and opportunities for companies.

Sometimes new information will highlight the increased riskiness of current company products and practices. For years, the tobacco industry ignored the evidence that had accumulated regarding the dangers of smoking. Similarly, opioid manufacturers are now paying billions in fines for ignoring data about the addictiveness of their products. Others simply have not thought about the risks. Equifax should have been aware of the increasing aggressiveness of hackers and dramatically increased its approach to security. A thorough scan of current practices and potentially damaging changes will help companies better prepare for the future.

INCREASE BOARD ACCOUNTABILITY FOR CORPORATE PURPOSE AND ETHICAL BEHAVIOR

One of the most glaring and persistent failures of today's corporate landscape is the behavior of most boards of directors. Many boards pay little attention to the social purpose or ethical behavior of the corporation. Like that of the CEO and the top-executive team, the board's attention is consistently overwhelmed by a focus on growth and profitability.

A new philosophy of board responsibility, in which the board is responsible not only to the shareholders but also to the corporate purpose itself, is emerging. The most effective boards review and affirm the corporate purpose, how management plans to balance that purpose with economic goals, and how management will create a culture that can serve all stakeholders.

Among the key roles the board plays in the achievement of corporate purpose is the hiring of a CEO who is a true moral leader and the examination of key strategies and corporate initiatives to determine whether they contribute to the corporate purpose and the company's ethical commitments. In addition, boards need to deliver more faithfully on existing commitments to monitor the company's ethics efforts and deal with cases of misconduct. Finally, the board needs to ensure that the company is detecting the emergence of new ethics risks in its own operations and in the environment.

To exercise the board's responsibilities for managing corporate purpose and ethical behavior, every board, perhaps through a committee, should take a deep dive into the ethical quality of the company's current strategy, the ongoing ethics risks of that strategy, and the company's risk of future ethical misconduct. This will require a detailed understanding of the company's ethical culture and its recent ethical performance, neither of which is currently available to most boards.

REFORM EXISTING ETHICS AND COMPLIANCE PROGRAMS

Now we come to the practices companies have long employed to create and sustain ethical culture. An effective ethics and compliance program, as addressed at length in chapter 3, is a key bulwark against misconduct in the organization. In chapter 3, the twelve most common practices of such programs were enumerated, and their typical weaknesses were identified.

Corporate leaders must commit to the reform and improvement of these standard practices. Ethics officers generally are aware of the weaknesses of their own programs but are hampered in their attempts to strengthen the programs by the preeminence of shareholder interests, the opposition of many line managers, selective attention from most executive suites and boardrooms, and by limited budgets.

These programs are also constrained by a corporate attitude that they are merely cost centers, contributing little to the accomplishment of the company's purpose. As a result, most companies are guilty of gross underinvestment in programs to shape the ethical corporate culture.

Companies and their ethics and compliance staffs must improve their implementation of the twelve corporate practices outlined in chapter 3. The programs must emphasize not just compliance but also ethics and the new focus on the corporation's social purpose.

But there are several specific ways the practices must be changed to do a better job of reducing corporate misconduct. These include the following:

Employee Ethics and Compliance Training Built on Corporate Purpose and Detailed Ethical Commitments. The company's purpose and ethical principles must be at the core of all ethics and compliance training. If this is not the case, then training is simply an exercise in checking the box required by the US sentencing guidelines.

Three principles should drive effective training. First, the primary purpose should be to understand the implications and applications of the company's purpose and ethical commitments, not just the compliance standards that can be stated as bright-line rules. Second, the training must be so tailored that all employees know what the company's beliefs mean for their own work—how a customer call is handled, how a product is designed, how the supply chain is managed, and how the shop floor is organized, for example. Third, the training must be a dialogue between management and employees on how the purpose and ethical commitments can be achieved in the day-to-day work of the company. In some circumstances, employees are going to know more than supervisors and managers about where ethical challenges arise.

Middle-Management Ethics Training. To enable line executives and middle managers to deliver on the new accountability outlined earlier, a new kind of ethics and compliance training must be provided. Corporate culture is built on motivating middle managers to be the ambassadors of the purpose and values of the company and its culture.

Line executives and middle managers must be trained to translate the company's purpose into detailed ethical commitments and clear goals for their individual units. This may require detailed discussions involving top management about the meaning of the social purpose and how the social and economic goals are to be balanced. Goal setting requires more sophisticated key performance indicators, and effective communication of these goals to all employees requires a different kind of management skill.

A New Approach to Hiring and Onboarding. New employees can strengthen or weaken a corporate culture. Companies have the opportunity to strengthen or weaken the corporate culture through the hiring process. It is critical to include considerations of values and integrity in hiring, as we discussed in chapter 2. Better methods must be developed to screen for values and what we earlier referred to as *ethical strength*, the ability to resist pressure and incentives to do the wrong thing.

Once new employees are hired, the onboarding process—increasingly recognized as a critical organizational function—must focus to a greater extent on the values and ethical commitments of the specific corporate culture. Most onboarding programs give only token attention to the purposes and ethics of the company. Often, employees are handed a copy of the corporate values statement or code of conduct and merely asked to sign a statement that they received it. This gives a clear message that the standards of conduct are unimportant and merely a matter of compliance.

The most important thing that can be done in onboarding is for the direct manager or supervisor of a new employee to discuss in some depth how the social purpose and ethical commitments of the company apply to the specific work of the unit the employee is joining.

Addressing Employee Misconduct. When companies uncover misconduct among current employees, they must be decisive in putting them on probation if they are salvageable and terminating them if they are not. Addressing misconduct that is not specifically tied to a compliance standard is more difficult. Companies need to develop the capacity to coach and discipline employees who got the balance wrong between economic goals and ethical commitments, even when there is not a specific compliance violation involved.

The discipline meted out to misbehaving employees is as important for the signals it sends to others about the acceptability of certain types of behavior as it is to protecting the company from the employee who misbehaved. Companies cannot be perceived as tolerating bad apples, no matter their status or economic contribution to the company. A few good examples of senior executives or contributors who were disciplined or fired can help an organization bring its commitment to life. So, obviously, can stories about employees and managers who had the courage to stand up for the purpose and principles.

IMPROVING CORPORATE ETHICAL PERFORMANCE

The goal of improving corporate ethical performance and reducing the likelihood of corporate misconduct is achievable, but it

---

EXHIBIT 5-1

IMMEDIATE ACTIONS COMPANIES CAN TAKE TO BETTER MANAGE CORPORATE ETHICS

1. Write and publish a **statement of corporate purpose** that goes beyond maximizing shareholder wealth.
2. Start describing how **key strategies and initiatives pursue the purposes** of the organization.
3. Set a dramatically **new tone at the top** as a moral leader.
4. Demand that **line managers take responsibility for purpose** and ethics.
5. Give the company's ethics office **a chance to weigh in on macro-ethics questions**.
6. Foster a **company environment** that is truly transparent and safe for employees.
7. Order an **audit of all company incentive plans and systems** to determine their ethics effects.
8. **Create a new scanning unit** to identify ethics impacts and risks.
9. **Establish board processes to monitor purpose and ethics** more closely.
10. **Tune up existing ethics program practices,** particularly:
    - **Redesign employee ethics training** to incorporate purpose and specific ethical commitments.
    - **Equip middle managers to take on accountability** for purpose and ethics.
    - **Encourage more extensive ethics-based hiring** and onboarding.
    - **Rehabilitate or terminate employees who misbehave.**

---

requires new strategies as well as improvements in the standard corporate ethics programs common in companies today. Our recommendations for immediate action by companies and their leaders are summarized in exhibit 5-1.

In short, corporate leaders need to adopt a corporate purpose that gives social contribution a standing along with economic goals. Leaders need to give the same time and attention to purpose and ethics as they do to other aspects of corporate activity. They need to successfully navigate the complicated challenge of balancing social purpose with economic goals. And they need to help each unit in the company to understand what the company's commitments mean to the work of that unit.

As business school professors and corporate consultants, we understand well the need to sustain and improve corporate profitability. But the persistence of corporate misconduct leads us to conclude that companies are badly underinvesting in their own ethics programs. CEOs who think that delivering a token statement or even a strong proclamation on the importance of ethics will make a difference are badly mistaken. An entirely new approach is needed—or the sorry litany of corporate misconduct will continue.

CHAPTER 6

Evaluating Ethical Risk and Performance

Are there particular companies that are prone to incidents of misconduct and scandal? Can we predict whether a company we are about to go to work for, do business with, invest in, or live next to will engage in bad behavior?

This chapter presents three tools to help answer these important questions. Executives, current and potential employees, investors, neighbors, and even regulators and public officials all have a stake in knowing when a company is an ethics risk.

The first tool, the **Ethical Performance Audit**, is a backward-looking evaluation of a company's past ethical performance and capability. What has been the company's record of ethical performance in the past? And what is the current strength of the company's efforts to manage ethical behavior?

The second tool, the **Ethical Risk Audit**, is a forward-looking approach, identifying companies that are likely to engage in misconduct and what type of misconduct may occur. It evaluates whether a company is crisis-prone or crisis-prepared. Taking past performance and current capability into account, this audit assesses the risk of future ethical violations.

The third tool, the **Sin-Dex**, helps with the processes of both looking back and looking forward. It measures which scandals or incidents of misconduct are the most serious. It can also aid the company's own efforts to evaluate ethics risk by anticipating how serious a specific type of ethical failure might be.

THE ETHICAL PERFORMANCE AUDIT: EVALUATING PAST PERFORMANCE

Every stakeholder, from management itself to all who are affected by the operations of the company, needs to know how well a company has managed its conduct in the past. This look at the recent past and current capability is important in itself, but it will also help in the later evaluation of the risk that the company will misbehave in the future.

To conduct an Ethical Performance Audit, management or an outside consultant should consider the following questions and data:

MEASURES OF PAST AND CURRENT ETHICAL PERFORMANCE

1. What incidents of misconduct has the company experienced in recent years? How much damage and how much intentionality were involved?
2. How frequently has the company and/or its employees been cited by outside bodies for ethical or compliance violations?

3. How frequently has the company and/or its employ-
    ees been cited in internal complaints and reporting?
4. What frequency and severity of misconduct are
    evident in reports to the company's hotline and data
    collected through investigations?
5. What frequency and severity of bad apples, bad bar-
    rels, and bad orchards are apparent in past incidents
    of misconduct?
6. What is the general reputation of the company,
    particularly regarding its treatment of customers,
    employees, and the communities in which it operates?
7. How well does the company rate on standard mea-
    sures of ethical and social responsibility, includ-
    ing diversity, environmental impact, product and
    employee safety, and so forth?
8. How well does the company rate on platforms for
    reporting on ethics and social responsibility that the
    company participates in and supports?
9. How well does the company score on environmental,
    social, and governance (ESG) measures compiled by
    others from public sources?
10. What are the frequency and severity of activist
    pressures that have been directed at the company in
    recent years? The concerns of these activists, even if
    currently considered fringe or unreasonable, give an
    indication of future concerns and criticisms.

STRENGTH OF THE CORPORATE CULTURE AND SYSTEMS

1. Does the company commit itself to an explicit pur-
    pose? A purpose beyond profit maximization?

2. Are there systems, controls, and governance in place to implement the commitment to purpose?

3. Is the CEO a respected moral leader? Are other senior executives?

4. Does the company routinely review proposed strategies and new products and services for their ethical impact?

5. Does the company require accountability from line and middle managers for the achievement of corporate purpose and ethical commitments in their units?

6. Does the company review incentive plans and other systems for their effects on ethical conduct?

7. How effectively are the values and ethics of applicants and new hires evaluated, at both the managerial and hourly levels?

8. How effective are the systems for recognizing and dealing with problematic employees (bad apples)?

9. How good is the company at identifying subcultures within the company that are ethically problematic (bad barrels)?

10. How well does the company manage difficult external ethical environments (bad orchards)?

11. How good is the company at identifying emerging social and ethical concerns?

12. How complete and effective are the elements of the company's ethics and compliance program? (See chapters 3 and 5 for initiatives and practices.)

ATTITUDES AND OPINIONS OF THE EMPLOYEES
AND THEIR REPORTS OF ETHICS PROBLEMS

1. How aware are employees of the company's values and ethics commitments?
2. Do the employees believe the company actually operates by these values?
3. How much confidence do the employees have in the ethics of their unit and their own supervisors?
4. How much misconduct that employees observe in the company do they report?
5. Do employees believe they can freely and safely report misconduct without retaliation?
6. Do employees believe they can ask questions and express views about the ethics of company strategies, programs, products, and services?
7. How do employees rate the effectiveness of key elements in the company's ethics systems?

Rating corporate ethical performance is of significant value to the company. There are many different audit methods and survey instruments that can be used to gather the information for an Ethical Performance Audit. Some surveys are done by internal staff, others by external consultants or professional organizations. Sometimes companies can compare their performance to other company or industry data. They can also compare their performance year to year and track whether initiatives to improve ethical performance are successful. Auditing corporate ethical performance can identify critical gaps in performance. Quantifying performance levels on each measure with a simple system (e.g., a scale from 1 to 10) can provide the data needed for improvement over time.

It is typical that a company will do well on some aspects of ethical performance and not so well on others. By identifying the weaker areas and using the recommendations outlined in chapter 5, a company can greatly improve its ethical performance over time. No company wants to be highlighted in a future book on corporate misconduct!

THE ETHICAL RISK AUDIT: EVALUATING
THE RISK OF A FUTURE SCANDAL

Every stakeholder—executives, ethics officers, customers, business partners, employees, investors, and others—would like to know the likelihood that a company will engage in misconduct in the future. Besides evaluating a company's performance in the past, there are ways of assessing the risk of misconduct in the future. These forward-looking evaluations are of particular use to current management, prospective employees, investors, and regulators and enforcers.

RED-FLAG WARNINGS

Past scandals have pointed to several leading indicators—or red flags—giving warning that a company is particularly vulnerable to misconduct. These red flags should alert corporate executives and others that there may be undiscovered misconduct or at least the near-term possibility of misconduct. These red flags are summarized in exhibit 6-1. They are as follows:

Company Record of Repeated Misconduct. Companies cannot change their behavior overnight. A company caught in repeated misconduct—mistreatment of employees, disregard for human rights, poor compliance with environmental laws—is a bad barrel and has a culture that is likely to produce misconduct again. Companies can spend millions in the wake of a scandal to strengthen their ethics and compliance programs, but it is exceedingly difficult to change the culture sufficiently to head off repeat behavior.

Industry Record of Repeated Misconduct. As noted in chapter 4, operating in a bad orchard produces repeated pressures to engage in misconduct. Even if one company has so far evaded the misconduct common among its competitors, the pressures remain and may become more extreme over time. The company may face financial hardship that compromises its resolve to behave well. Changes in management may also weaken the internal resolve to resist misconduct.

The Imperial CEO. A culture resistant to ethical problems must be open and welcome information and input from all. The antithesis of this type of culture is one overseen by a CEO who does not tolerate criticism or information that challenges his or her chosen narrative and way of doing things. There are many examples of male CEOs who adopted an imperial style, but women are not exempt. Elizabeth Holmes of Theranos stands out as a female example. She styled herself as a superstar, the next Steve Jobs. She shut off any feedback that challenged the story of her success and influence.

A Star System for Promotions. Companies differ greatly on who gets promoted and what behaviors they exhibit. Some companies most reward those willing to risk everything to achieve a breakthrough win; others reward those who improve the units they manage more incrementally. A system that sees only the "big win," the financially risky behavior, as worthy of promotion will

EXHIBIT 6-1

RED-FLAG WARNINGS OF CRITICAL ETHICS RISKS

1. **Company Record of Repeated Misconduct**: The company has offended repeatedly and likely has a culture of disregard for ethics and standards.

2. **Industry Record of Repeated Misconduct**: Whether or not the company has repeatedly offended, its competitors have, thereby putting pressure on the firm.

3. **The Imperial CEO**: He or she cannot be challenged; the leader's image as a "star" insulates him or her from criticism or close scrutiny; the board just cheers at board meetings.

4. **A Star System for Promotions**: The most highly valued executives take big risks and have big wins; employees are "stars" or "losers."

5. **A Culture of Secrecy**: Information is held very tightly; even within the company, secrecy and distrust predominate.

6. **A Work-Around Culture**: The company expects goals to be achieved no matter what. There is an attitude of "don't tell me how you did it; just do it."

7. **Betting the Farm**: Company success is dependent on one product or technological breakthrough; the company cannot survive missing a deadline or the failure of a key product.

8. **Financially Distressed**: The company is on the ropes financially; the CEO's job is on the line if the company misses even a quarterly target.

9. **Lack of Oversight**: The board is not competent to provide oversight or is not engaged in active oversight; the board is often composed of celebrities, CEO friends, and so forth.

10. **Company Operates in Bad Orchards**: The company is active in localities rife with misconduct; there is concern about whether an ethical firm can successfully compete there.

inevitably create the incentive for leaders to increase the ethical risk in their organizations and to cover up their missteps.

A Culture of Secrecy. An ethically resilient company requires the free flow of information and the willingness of employees at all levels to raise concerns over questionable behavior. When information is excessively compartmentalized and employees are compelled to keep secrets, information on challenging situations or unethical behavior is not shared and frequently even suppressed. Secrecy also provides the opportunity to engage in and hide improper behaviors. Enforcing a culture of secrecy requires intimidating employees, which further erodes communication in the organization.

A Work-Around Culture. Some companies follow a philosophy of "do it by the book"; others foster what is known as a "work-around culture." The second type of company expects goals to be met despite any obstacles and may reward and praise those who accomplish goals by stretching the rules or engaging in misconduct. At its most extreme, a work-around culture openly encourages employees to get things done by doing anything they need to, as long as they do not get caught. Such cultures breed bribes, cheating, and violations of safety standards.

Betting the Farm. Some companies repeatedly bet the survival of the company on a single outcome—that a technological breakthrough will occur, that a major contract will be secured, that a single product will become a blockbuster, that a particular merger will be consummated. This puts inordinate pressure on every employee to meet the goals and timetables established, no matter what procedures or regulations they have to violate. This can also be the case with a particular division, sometimes headed by an executive caught in a "star system," as discussed previously. Most start-ups have bet-the-farm strategies. They are constantly at risk of failing, dependent on meeting targets or being shut down, and therefore are ethically vulnerable.

Financially Distressed. Some companies have significant reserves and borrowing capacity; others have used every dollar of cash and line of credit to invest in new opportunities, buy back stock, and fund huge executive bonuses. Just as there are large numbers of Americans who cannot come up with $400 for a car repair, many companies have little capacity to survive technological or market failures, economic downturns, or pandemic recessions. Some companies are backed into financial trouble by past failures; others embrace an extreme form of leverage that puts them at ethical risk.

Lack of Oversight. Governance in US corporations has long been troubled. Some boards are simply not doing their jobs; others are kept in the dark by management that does not want oversight. Many boards, even of some highly profitable firms, collect their fees and engage in nothing approaching good oversight. With weak governance, the danger of ethical misbehavior is greatly increased. Companies with weak governance typically permit more ethics risk to persist, and they may even tolerate unethical practices in the governance itself—such as blatant nepotism, related-party transactions, and unauthorized management actions.

Company Operates in Bad Orchards. Some companies are more exposed to ethical risk simply because they operate in industries or geographies that are ethically suspect. When the supply chain or a substantial portion of the sales occurs in corrupt and troubled environments, it is almost inevitable that misconduct of some type will occur. A company may reduce the frequency of violations, but accomplishing this requires significant investment and a willingness to walk away from questionable sales and sourcing arrangements.

A MORE THOROUGH ETHICAL RISK AUDIT

The red-flag indicators just described can usually be assessed by an individual who conscientiously reads the publicly available business and financial press. These indicators can provide a quick test of the need to protect yourself or your firm from a company prone to misconduct. These indicators can alert a college graduate or a potential hire that their own career may be held back by a crisis-prone organization.

A more thorough evaluation of future ethics risk, the kind a company should undertake, would involve assessing a more extensive series of questions that include the following:

DATA FROM THE MOST RECENT ETHICAL PERFORMANCE AUDIT

1. What are the frequency and severity of past behavior issues and past incidents of misconduct?
2. What is the strength of the corporate culture and systems for ethical issues?
3. What is the strength of the attitudes and beliefs of managers and employees on ethical issues?

LEARNING FROM THE ETHICS PERFORMANCE AUDIT AND PAST EXPERIENCE

1. How well has the company studied past patterns of misconduct and initiated new efforts to mitigate the risk that they will reoccur?
2. How well has the company identified the weaknesses in its corporate culture and systems and taken steps to improve them?

3. How well has the company listened to the attitudes
   and beliefs of managers and employees and initiated new programs and communications to increase
   understanding of the company's purpose and ethical
   commitments and confidence in its ethical systems?

RISKINESS OF THE CURRENT BUSINESS STRATEGY, FINANCIAL CONDITION, AND OPERATIONS

1. What are the ongoing "ethical impacts" of the company's products and services?
2. What ethical impacts of the company's products and
   services are not yet controversial but might become
   so if more information is revealed by the company or
   if public perceptions change dramatically?
3. What are the special ethics risks in the company's
   supply chain or business partnerships? How well does
   the company monitor these partner companies?
4. What incidents and pressures are being experienced
   by other firms in the same industry, by firms that
   produce similar products, or by firms that use similar
   methods of production or operation?
5. What is the likely impact of rogue companies in the
   industry whose neglect of standards will focus attention on all firms in the industry?
6. What is the likely impact of employees who have
   recently been acquired or who may not share the
   company's values? How good are the screening and
   onboarding procedures?
7. How exposed is the company to different ethical
   norms and practices around the world? How many

difficult environments does it operate in? What new
areas of operations—product markets or geographies—
is the company engaged in or considering? How ethically risky are these areas?

8. How much financial pressure for performance is the
    company under? Are specific units or work teams
    under particular pressure?

9. What criticisms have activist organizations or public
    officials leveled against the company or its industry?
    How does the company measure up in the areas of
    criticism?

THE COMPANY'S ABILITY TO MITIGATE ETHICS RISK

1. How aware is senior management of the company's
    ethical risks?

2. How aware is the board of directors of the company's
    ethical risks?

3. How effective is the company's system for addressing
    significant ethical risks?

4. How good is the company at detecting and managing
    bad apples?

5. How good is the company at understanding and shap-
    ing its ethical culture?

6. How good is the company at mitigating risk in chal-
    lenging environments?

7. How good is the company at dealing quickly and
    openly with incidents of misconduct?

8. How well managed is the company in general?

The evaluation of ethics risk is becoming a core skill for any successful company. Each organization must use both the red-flag indicators outlined previously and a more thorough method of evaluating its evolving ethics risks. And of course, the company must be aggressive in addressing the risks identified—reducing them where possible and putting strong measures in place to head off misconduct in areas of risk.

THE SIN-DEX: EVALUATING THE PAST, EMERGING, AND POTENTIAL SCANDALS

To know how serious past misconduct and violations were—and how much of a risk possible future misconduct is—the company and all its stakeholders need a way of measuring the seriousness of incidents of misconduct. One such tool is the Sin-Dex, which we have used to evaluate how much impact misconduct has had on the company's stakeholders but also to determine what kind of moral blame companies bear for this misconduct.

The Sin-Dex is a scale that measures the severity of any past incident of corporate misconduct and gives critical guidance regarding the significance of emerging scandals a company is managing. It can aid in the evaluation of the ethical risks of proposed strategies and initiatives.

Business leaders, regulators and law enforcement, investors, and employees need a way to distinguish between routine or minor incidents of misconduct and major incidents that produce public and government concern, which disrupt the company and even threaten its existence. To do this in a quantifiable way, the Sin-Dex gives each incident of misconduct or potential misconduct a rating from 0 to 10. The worst corporate actions as measured by this Sin-Dex should get the priority attention of corporate executives and ethics officers trying to reduce the incidence of misconduct, as well as policy makers shaping future regulations and penalties. The sanctions for the most serious corporate actions should be the most severe.

The Sin-Dex categorizes the severity of scandals or incidents of corporate misconduct on two scales: how much actual or potential *damage* the scandal does and how much *intentionality* motivated the behavior. Prosecutors and judges deal with both damage and intentionality in deciding what crimes to charge wrongdoers with and in setting financial and criminal penalties for wrongful behavior.

By understanding the severity of misbehavior, it becomes easier to focus corporate and public efforts to remediate and prevent the most serious events and to make greater efforts to prevent the reoccurrence of a similar incident. By understanding how intentional a particular scandal is, we get a clearer understanding of how to stop the behavior going forward.

Ethical risk assessment focuses on both the likelihood of misconduct and also the severity of the possible misconduct, which the Sin-Dex evaluates. Corporate leaders need this information to create an effective ethics and compliance program. Board members need it to provide oversight in the most critical areas. Middle managers and supervisors need it to better mitigate risks in their own operations.

The Sin-Dex identifies five levels of *damage* and five levels of *intentionality* that distinguish the most serious incidents of corporate misconduct from the less serious.

DAMAGE

The five levels of damage or risk of damage are as follows:

Level 5: Loss of human life, severe injuries, or likelihood
of such damage

Level 4: Significant injury, substantial financial damage
to a stakeholder, or meaningful disruption in personal
lives

Level 3: Moderate injury or damage to the financial welfare of a stakeholder

Level 2: Minor injury or damage to the financial welfare
of a stakeholder

Level 1: Only incidental damage to the financial welfare of
a stakeholder

Level 0: No damage or risk of damage to any stakeholder

The damage rating should be modified if corporate misconduct
imposes costs on hundreds or thousands of customers, employees,
or other stakeholders rather than just a few. Obviously, the greater
the number of lives lost or of individuals whose financial welfare
has been damaged, the more serious the incident. As noted, the
scale can be used to evaluate both past misconduct and the potential damage from future misconduct.

The scale counts putting lives *at risk* as seriously as actually
causing the loss of life. Sometimes companies are just lucky that
misconduct does not result in actual damage. Boeing's misconduct
in the design of pilot software appears to have led to the loss of two
airplanes full of passengers, but other equally risky decisions may
not have caused a crash. Arguably, both cases would be rated as
severe on the damage scale.

We have used the disruption of the lives of stakeholders as a part of the definition of damage at levels 1–4. It is important to recognize the second-order effects of corporate misconduct. Wells Fargo's sales team may not have done much immediate damage by the creation of fake accounts, but the disruption of the financial lives of the customers affected caused them to have cars repossessed, to lose opportunities to buy homes as a result of low credit scores, to lose jobs, and so forth. These are severe damages.

INTENTION

On this key measure, how intentional the action was, the five levels are as follows:

Level 5: Action is deliberate and premeditated; it is done with the involvement or full knowledge of one or more senior executives.

Level 4: Action is deliberate; it is done with the involvement or knowledge of supervisors or managers at a level below the senior executive team.

Level 3: Action is deliberate; it results from tolerance by supervisors or related patterns of behavior being rewarded by the organizational culture.

Level 2: Action is deliberate; damage results from neglect of good standards or good management processes.

Level 1: Action is deliberate; damage results from a low-probability event despite having a reasonable standard of prevention.

Level 0: Action is unintentional; it is truly accidental, due to random error, not poor policy, systems, or neglect.

The intention scale recognizes that deliberate actions that result in damage are more serious. But it also recognizes that deliberate actions can be undertaken at various levels of foreseeable risk. Levels 3 and 4 are deliberate actions taken with the knowledge of supervisors or senior management. Level 2 acknowledges that some damage results from neglect rather than direct intent, whereas level 1 suggests there is always some risk of damage present but that the company has made reasonable efforts to reduce the risk. Level 0 damage results from causes that could not have been foreseen.

Exhibit 6-2 provides a visual representation of the Sin-Dex.

The Sin-Dex enables executives and outsiders to refine their understanding of ethics risk by more closely examining the blame they will bear if misconduct is revealed. The more serious the potential misconduct, the more effort the company should put into reducing the risk. When a corporate scandal emerges, such a measure can help the public, including the media, determine how serious the misconduct is. It can alert corporate leadership to the urgency of a response. In the aftermath of misconduct, such a measure can help regulators and courts determine fines and penalties.

The Sin-Dex determines the level of *moral responsibility* management bears for a scandal or misconduct that has occurred. The most severe cases on either scale are significant threats to public welfare. Because it evaluates the moral responsibility for the misconduct, it is also a reasonable predictor of public interest and outrage over the incident, as well as regulatory and legislative action. It may also measure the risk that the misconduct may reoccur in the future without remedial action.

We have combined the two measures to create a shorthand *index number* from the Sin-Dex by adding the two numbers. A "5,5" for example, gets the highest rating, 10, and should be the

EXHIBIT 6-2

THE SIN-DEX

	DAMAGE	INTENTION
5	Loss of human life, severe injuries, or likelihood of such damage	Action is deliberate and premeditated; done with involvement or full knowledge of one or more senior executives
4	Significant injury, substantial financial damage to a stakeholder, or meaningful disruption in personal lives	Action is deliberate; involvement by management at a level below the senior executive team
3	Moderate injury or damage to the financial welfare of a stakeholder	Action is deliberate; results from tolerance of or rewards for related bad behavior
2	Minor injury or damage to the financial welfare of a stakeholder	Action is deliberate; damage results from neglect of good standards or good management
1	Only incidental damage to the financial welfare of a stakeholder	Action is deliberate; damage results from a low-probability event despite having a reasonable standard of prevention
0	No damage or risk of damage to any stakeholder	Action is unintentional; truly accidental, due to random error, not poor policy, systems, or neglect

most worrying type of misconduct we encounter. It puts human life at risk, and it does so as a result of a deliberate decision by senior management. On the other hand, a "1,1" represents an action that does only incidental damage and was undertaken with an acceptable amount of care.

For example, the failure of engineers at General Motors to properly label replacement parts led to more than 125 deaths of motorists, according to the company's own resolution process. This clearly puts this scandal at a level 5 on the damage scale. The intention was not to kill but to save money in response to corporate pressure for profits. This puts the intentionality at a level 3, leading to an overall rating of 8.

In contrast, Wells Fargo's fake accounts scandal affected hundreds of thousands of customers, disrupting their financial and personal lives, but did not directly threaten human life. The damage would normally rate a 3, but given the thousands of customers affected, we would raise it to at least a 4. The intention, however, was clear and widespread throughout the company, earning a score of 4. Thus, the overall rating would be an 8.

The actions of Massey Energy and its leader, Don Blankenship, which led to the 2010 mine explosion that killed twenty-nine miners, arguably should be rated a 10. Blankenship, prosecutors argued, deliberately created a culture where safety violations and past accidents were ignored or violated, and a clandestine system to alert workers during federal mine inspector visits was put in place.

Exhibit 6-3 presents ratings for the most prominent scandals discussed in this book.

Any incident of misconduct that is rated 4 or higher should automatically be a cause for corporate and public concern. Any incident with a 3 rating, or a 2 rating on the damage scale alone, should be cause for investigation and remediation. Any incident rated 3 or above on the intention scale alone should provoke significant changes in policy and procedure.

In any rating system, there are likely to be disagreements about the precise number given. But the Sin-Dex can help with gaining at least a general understanding of the severity of a scandal or an incident of corporate misconduct and the intention or cause. A

EXHIBIT 6-3

SIN-DEX RATINGS OF RECENT INCIDENTS OF CORPORATE MISCONDUCT

SCANDAL	BEHAVIOR	DAMAGE	INTENTION	RATING
Volkswagen	Installation of defeat devices	5	5	10
Massey Mines	Repeated mine disasters	5	5	10
Peanut Corporation	*Salmonella* outbreak	5	5	10
Rana Plaza	Unsafe working conditions, 1,134 killed	5	5	10
BP	Lax safety leads to oil spill	5	4	9
Enron	Financial fraud	4	5	9
Theranos	Promoting/installing fake products	4	5	9
Boeing	Installation of unsafe software	5	4	9
Satyam Computer	Financial manipulation and fraud	4	5	9
Takata	Cost cutting leads to unsafe airbags	5	3	8
Wells Fargo	Creation of fake customer accounts	4	4	8
Blue Bell Creameries	Contaminated food	5	3	8
Airbus	Widespread bribery to sell planes	3	5	8
Embraer	Bribery to sell planes	3	5	8
Barings Bank	Fraud by unit general manager	4	4	8
JP Morgan	Hiring children of Chinese officials	2	5	7
Equifax	Massive breach of data	3	3	6

rating system can build awareness of misconduct, its origins, and its impact. A rating system can encourage improved management and accountability within the company, lest it be guilty of a highly rated scandal.

One of the other significant benefits of any rating or performance measurement system is the process of rating and discussions around the ratings. Even though ratings are often imprecise, they create an opportunity for management discussions toward improvement.

There are other difficulties with a scale or index of any type, of course. Sometimes the damage done is known with precision. At other times, we do not know the extent of the damage done or the intent behind the incident, particularly in the days or weeks immediately after a scandal emerges. Nevertheless, we do get early indications that allow a rough evaluation of the scale of the misconduct.

Some scandals will have a change in their rating as more is known about them, whereas a few stand out as a 10 from the beginning. The Bernard Madoff scandal, in which it was quickly determined that his investment firms were little more than a Ponzi scheme, was directed from the top and had done immense financial damage to a large number of investors.

Other scandals emerge slowly and climb the rating scale. The explosion of a gas pipeline in San Bruno, California, which led to nine deaths, provoked questions regarding the maintenance and monitoring practices of the local utility Pacific Gas and Electric (PG&E). Extensive investigations determined that the pipeline that exploded was not maintained properly and that the utility did not even have records to determine when it had been serviced. Over time, the severity escalated as the threat to individuals near any of the company's other poorly maintained pipelines was determined to be serious. Later scandals over the involvement of PG&E electrical lines in the origin of several fatal Northern California fires made it clear that the management neglect was deliberate and widespread.

The Sin-Dex has many critical uses. It provides a useful guide to questions that should be asked to investigate how serious any misconduct is. Corporate leadership, as well as regulators, will want to know the cause of each incident, particularly how much top management was involved or aware of the problem. Research on the impact will help determine how widespread and substantial the damage is. This helps corporate leadership, as well as outside authorities, to respond effectively to corporate misconduct.

HOW COMPANIES AND OTHER STAKEHOLDERS CAN USE THESE THREE TOOLS

The three tools presented in this chapter are immediately useful for companies that want to improve their management of ethics and compliance and reduce their risk of misconduct. The tools can highlight areas of ethical performance that need to be strengthened and help companies track improvement over time. They can also identify the riskiness of new areas of business and new strategies being pursued. But the tools are useful for others as well.

Investors have a significant stake in the ethical performance and capabilities of the companies in their portfolios. Incidents of misconduct can affect stock price, weaken the confidence of employees and other stakeholders in the company, lead to a drop in sales, and make government permits and approvals harder to obtain.

To date, few investors have relied on public reputational surveys to flag the most serious ethical risks in their portfolios. This is clearly not adequate for the future. Environmental risk, one dimension of ethics risk, has already begun to affect stock prices. If a company has many properties that will be affected by sea-level rise, flooding, or heat waves—all expected in the next twenty-five years—then that should be reflected in the stock price. So, too, should a company's capability to address the environmental aspects of its own operations and participate in a global solution to the climate crisis.

ESG evaluations, ratings that evaluate the environmental, social, and governance performance of companies, are increasingly available to all investors and the public. They are performed by firms offering data and funds geared to investors' values and tolerance for risk. Companies are under increasing pressure to reveal their scores on some of these common data platforms. Typically, such platforms permit the company to compare its data to national or global averages or, in some cases, to their specific industry.

The tools in this chapter can also enable current and potential employees to recognize the most problematic corporations to work for. There is increasing evidence that employees are taking a company's values, ethical commitments, and record into account when seeking employment. Employees aiming to manage the risk that they may be involved with a corrupt or ethically problematic company often only have access to personal observations and anecdotes from others. Employees in functions other than product engineering at Boeing, Takata, or Volkswagen, for example, may not have been able to see the scandals coming—likewise for non-sales employees at Wells Fargo and nonmanufacturing employees at Blue Bell Creameries or Peanut Corporation of America. More transparency can help employees make better choices in the future.

For the policy maker, an understanding of the ethical risk of a particular company or industry can greatly aid the

policy-development process. Heavier criminal and financial penalties may provide a disincentive in areas where misbehavior is
likely. Increased or targeted regulatory standards or enforcement
may be warranted in areas where policy makers conclude that misconduct is unavoidable because of the overwhelming incentives for
it. Changing the playing field may head off the misbehavior we can
anticipate.

CHAPTER 7

Can We Stop All Corporate Misconduct?

Stopping all corporate misconduct is too ambitious a goal, but the collective efforts of corporate leaders and many others can reduce its frequency, rein in the most damaging incidents, and restore greater confidence in this imperfect capitalist system.

Stopping corporate misconduct is not solely the job of corporate executives. Policy makers have a critical role to play in passing laws and writing regulations that prohibit the worst behavior and establish guardrails. Moral educators—in families, churches, and schools—can reduce the number of bad apples in companies by providing good moral educations, modeling moral behaviors, and creating communities that support doing the right thing. Business school educators like ourselves can do a better job of teaching the importance of corporate purpose and moral leadership and the most effective managerial methods for leading an ethical company.

The general public and the media have a role to play as well. Corporate misconduct must never be perceived as inevitable or acceptable. It cannot be dismissed as a tolerable cost of economic activity. We must demand that the companies dominating our economy serve *all* their stakeholders. The media must track corporate behavior closely and expose substandard behavior. Activists must highlight patterns of behavior that need to be addressed. Ordinary citizens should call out improper conduct on social media when they see it.

This chapter identifies key initiatives the rest of us can take that will complement the reforms business is adopting to manage its ethical behavior for the better.

BETTER LAWS AND REGULATIONS TO PREVENT MISCONDUCT

We believe any effort to reduce the frequency of corporate misconduct must include a more complete set of laws and regulations to address the many problematic dimensions of corporate misbehavior. More rigorous enforcement of the laws and regulations already enacted, stronger and more consistent punishments for individual and corporate perpetrators of business misbehavior, and the occasional imprisonment of employees and executives who violate standards would be beneficial.

We do not believe the answer is to write a law or regulation for every possible violation. It is impossible to write a bright-line rule for every type of possible misconduct. Even if it were possible, the excessive accumulation of compliance standards would sap some of the energy and innovation from the economic system. But there are many new areas, particularly in the emerging world of technology, where regulation is critical. In general, laws and regulations should address those cases where misconduct will be particularly damaging to some group, such as customers or the community, or where the incentives to engage in misconduct will produce "a race to the bottom" as companies cut costs to compete.

STRONGER MORAL EDUCATION

Our analysis of bad apples in chapter 2 suggests many business people today think only about their own self-interests and that of their shareholders, neglecting concerns they might demonstrate as responsible human beings in private life. The values revolution, which some have called for in corporate life, must come first in our broader society. Moral education must be reinvigorated to encourage individuals of conscience to step up and help companies act ethically.

First, moral education must be restored and renewed in K–12 schools. Some teachers and school administrators have hesitated to stand up for important principles and call out the behavior of individual students (and educators) who have misbehaved. A pernicious ethic of "do your own thing" and unrestrained freedom is a legacy of the last fifty years. To their credit, some Gen Xers and millennials are insisting on values embracing diversity and the need for environmental reforms that ought to be part of any necessary values initiative. Educators must fight the normalization of bullying, demonization of others, and untruthfulness emanating from the political world.

Churches are fighting for relevance as their congregations shrink. By developing the expertise to address complex ethical questions facing their congregants who work in business and other fields, they may be able to reestablish themselves as pillars of the community. But first, they can set a strong moral example by dealing with misconduct in their own organizations.

Business schools, where we have spent a good portion of our lives, must challenge the dominance of the economic model affirming that shareholder wealth is the only concern of business. To prepare the moral leaders of tomorrow, faculty must document the shifts in corporate purpose toward serving all stakeholders, how companies address the many ethical challenges they face, and how they create and sustain an ethical culture.

MORE HELP FOR COMPANIES DEALING WITH BAD ORCHARDS

We are sympathetic to cases where executives must cope with environments that are difficult to operate in ethically. But as noted earlier, we are not sympathetic to executives who excuse their own misconduct by arguing they are simply "leveling the playing field."

One solution is writing extraterritorial laws and regulations. This would establish clear guidelines that unacceptable conduct at home is unacceptable abroad too. Extraterritorial laws can also bind foreign companies that have operations in the United States or the United Kingdom, thereby setting global ethical standards for some sectors of business. More aggressive enforcement of these laws can help.

Beyond enforcement, companies need to align themselves with collective efforts—promoting anti-corruption, human rights, and environmental responsibility—in countries where they do business. In addition, private agreements to eschew bribery, where permitted by antitrust law, can help keep particular bidding processes cleaner. Strengthening the corporation's own ethical culture, following the steps outlined in chapter 5, is obviously a key strategy as well.

As noted in chapter 4, there are some difficult environments where companies cannot operate ethically and survive economically. Companies need to have the integrity to stay out of such environments so as not to contaminate their own efforts to sustain ethical cultures inside the company.

GREATER PUBLIC AND MEDIA SCRUTINY OF BUSINESS BEHAVIOR

We believe the chances of motivating companies to take the significant actions outlined in this book will be increased if the public is watching closely. While corporation-bashing is currently in fashion, and some interests are eager to use every new corporate scandal as a reason to abandon capitalism and free markets, we believe the long-term survival of capitalism actually demands close public and media scrutiny of corporate behavior.

We think a public understanding of the character and causes of corporate misconduct will help companies in the long term, as well as encourage them to follow through on the initiatives designed to reduce misconduct. Some segments of the public have become complacent about corporate scandals because too many people think misconduct is inevitable. Likewise, too many stories of misconduct are written by reporters and commentators unfamiliar with the workings of business. We need investigative stories on scandals, particularly those involving complex and global decision-making. Reporters must be able to not only penetrate the corporate explanations that blame all misconduct on bad apples or bad orchards but also resist the temptation to condemn every corporate action as ill-intentioned.

We believe a more informed public and media will be able to tell major incidents of misconduct (9s and 10s on our Sin-Dex) from minor missteps (1s or 2s). Similarly, they will come to differentiate good from bad responses to misconduct that occurs. Heightened scrutiny can motivate the right kind of business behavior. Companies will want to give attention to steps that will create a more ethical culture and will act more quickly when misconduct is discovered.

We know many corporate executives argue that public opinion and outrage are out of control, that well-meaning managers and executives are being singled out unfairly. We don't think so. We believe greater attention to misconduct and to the specific named perpetrators will lead to greater trust in corporate behavior.

CLEARER STANDARDS FOR HOW COMPANIES SHOULD HANDLE MISCONDUCT

Much of the damage inflicted by corporate misconduct occurs after the misbehavior is first discovered. It is critical to set a new standard for how companies handle incidents of misconduct. Not all misconduct can be prevented, but it is possible to limit the damage done to people and the environment in its wake.

We believe companies have been particularly lax in managing the aftermath of misconduct. Companies do not want to blow the whistle on themselves, so they frequently suppress information about misconduct or suspected misbehavior. They sometimes decide not to investigate an accusation or a likely case because they would rather not know the real story.

Recent federal investigative procedures have created incentives for companies to investigate misconduct themselves and share their findings openly. This is helpful, but there must be a clear standard of good corporate behavior in the face of scandal.

The key steps in an adequate response to an emerging incident of misconduct, as outlined in exhibit 7-1, are as follows:

Discover the Problem. The first step is for the firm to detect the misconduct itself at the first possible moment. The company

---

EXHIBIT 7-1

SETTING A STANDARD FOR CORPORATE RESPONSE TO MISCONDUCT

1. **Discover the problem.**
2. **Provide immediate aid to victims.**
3. **Investigate how it occurred.**
4. **Be transparent at every step.**
5. **Execute an effective remedial plan.**
6. **Continue public disclosure for the long term.**

---

should discover safety and quality problems in products before consumers point them out. Internal hotlines should quickly alert the company to misconduct by individual employees or units.

Managers and executives at every level in the firm should be responsible for identifying misconduct in their own organization. Information should be shared quickly with top management and the board. Companies need a zero-tolerance policy toward attempts to hide problems in the organization. When Wells Fargo executives discovered the unethical behavior encouraged by the cross-selling initiative, they chose to simply ignore it. The cost of that decision now numbers in the billions.

Provide Immediate Aid to Victims. The second step is to protect the victims of misconduct immediately. If customers are using faulty products, the company needs to have an aggressive recall program. If a manager or the general culture has been discriminating against women or certain racial groups, the company should act quickly to make things right for the individuals affected. Johnson & Johnson's handling of the 1982 Tylenol poisonings remains an exemplar of this kind of proactive response.

Sometimes, identifying the victims can be a costly exercise. BP had an obligation to provide immediate assistance to the families of the workers killed on the Deepwater Horizon platform, but it also spent millions to identify those who were economically harmed by the Gulf oil spill and then billions to compensate them. The goodwill afforded by these payments, though, helped BP weather a storm of its own making.

Investigate How It Occurred. The third step is to investigate exactly what happened and why. Good managers move immediately to investigate misconduct or identify the causes. Other managers, embarrassed by what has occurred, have preferred to sweep it under the rug and blame the problem on a few bad apples or an outside force.

Without an effective investigation, the company may retain an employee who will misbehave again, continue to use a system that encourages misconduct, or go on selling a product that is unsafe or unreliable.

Be Transparent at Every Step. The fourth step is to report publicly and frequently about what is known—the nature of the misconduct, the damage done, and the status of the investigation. Transparency is critical to enable those who feel threatened to protect themselves. A lack of transparency indicates an unwillingness by the company to subject itself to public scrutiny.

In a well-documented incident several years ago, Odwalla, a beverage company, handled the inadvertent poisoning of one of its products by conducting a rapid investigation and holding a daily news conference to reveal all the company knew about the case. Despite one death and many serious injuries, Odwalla was credited for handling the poisoning well and changing its processes immediately. Unsurprisingly, Odwalla's brand survived the crisis.

Execute an Effective Remedial Plan. The fifth step is the remedial action. Besides conducting an effective investigation that identifies the true cause of the misconduct, organizations need to act quickly to discipline or remove the individuals involved, change the systems and incentives that led to the misbehavior, and put additional monitoring in place to ensure the causes are resolved.

The response of the US Conference of Catholic Bishops (USCCB) to the child-abuse scandals affecting hundreds of priests and thousands of victims demonstrates a failure at each of these first five steps. The USCCB is accused of doing everything wrong—failing to investigate, covering up the misconduct, protecting the perpetrators, not supporting the victims, and in some cases using overly aggressive legal tactics to reduce financial exposure for remediation.

The test of a good remedial plan, of course, is that the problem does not reoccur. Only then can the public begin to trust that the company or organization is effectively managing the problem.

Continue Public Disclosure for the Long Term. The sixth step is long-term public disclosure. A company must report periodically and publicly over several years about its remedial actions and their effects. The press will want to revisit the incident; potential victims will want the reassurance that they are protected. Members of the public will want to know if they can place their trust in this company again.

Establishing the six actions just described as corporate best practice will reduce the damage from incidents of misconduct and reduce the likelihood that the misconduct will reoccur.

CAN WE PREVENT ALL CORPORATE MISCONDUCT?

Having chronicled and analyzed the persistent problem of rotten corporate conduct over the past fifty years, we need to ask if there is any realistic strategy to prevent *all* misconduct. Our shorthand answer to this question is no.

Still, we believe that the initiatives outlined in this book can greatly reduce the frequency and damage of such behavior. We believe we can significantly reduce the frequency of corporate misconduct if business leaders take their responsibilities to manage the ethical purpose, character, and goals of the firm seriously. And if the rest of us support the additional measures outlined in this chapter.

We reject the two solutions some of the most radical critics propose: writing a law or regulation to govern every action a company takes and passing ownership of business to the state. But we also reject the belief that nothing can be done to reduce misconduct and the damage it causes.

Abandoning capitalism and turning over responsibility for economic activity to the state is no solution. Patterns of misconduct are as common in government agencies and public bodies as they are in corporations. The solution, in our view, is in creating effective regulations and the right incentives for those in private business to behave better.

No matter the solution, though, we cannot continue to accept the current level of misconduct. Too much damage is being done to people and their interests, and to the economy itself. The strategies in this book give us the chance to reduce rotten behavior significantly without abandoning the vitality of our market system.

CASE STUDIES

EXHIBITS

ACKNOWLEDGMENTS

In academic and consulting careers that have spanned the 1970–2020 period, the authors have incurred many debts—for professional, intellectual, and spiritual inspiration and assistance. Our own insights and concepts are built on the pioneering work of so many others in the fields of business ethics, corporate social responsibility and sustainability, accounting, organizational development, character development, leadership, and governance.

We are grateful to the CEOs, executives, board members, ethics officers, employees, and others in companies who have provided valuable examples of and insights on the causes of corporate misconduct, as well as best practices to avoid and mitigate rotten corporate behavior. Many have faced challenging decisions with great integrity, recognizing the critical importance of ethical decision-making. They have inspired us and helped us understand the importance and possibility of improving corporations and society. It is our hope that through this book, we may do the same for others.

Besides their inspiration, these corporate leaders have given us a more complete understanding of top management's perspective; a better appreciation of the challenges managers at all levels face; and significant insight into the role of managerial processes, corporate governance, and ethical leadership in improving corporate ethical performance and reducing corporate misconduct. They have generously shared both their successes and their failures.

We are also very grateful to the universities that have been our academic homes. And we are particularly indebted to the many academic colleagues and students over the years with whom we have discussed and debated the ideas presented here. We thank them for their contributions. The conclusions and the critical perspectives presented in this book are ours alone, of course, although many views would be shared by our colleagues in academia and in the corporate world.

This book is dedicated to our families. Without their patience and support, it could not have been completed. They have provided many ideas for this book, but also emotional support, affection, love, inspiration, and joy throughout our careers. Our lives are more complete and fulfilled because of them. To them, we offer our love and deepest appreciation.

ABOUT THE AUTHORS

MARC J. EPSTEIN was, until recently, Distinguished Research Professor of Management at Jones Graduate School of Business at Rice University in Houston, Texas. Prior to joining Rice, Dr. Epstein was a professor at Stanford Graduate School of Business, Harvard Business School, and INSEAD (European Institute of Business Administration).

With extensive academic research and practical experience in the implementation of corporate strategies and the development of performance metrics, Dr. Epstein is considered one of the global leaders in the areas of corporate governance, social and environmental sustainability, performance measurement and management, and corporate accountability. He has also written extensively on corporate misconduct and accountants' legal liability and ethics, innovation, organizational trust, and corporate social and environmental impacts.

He is the author of twenty books and well over two hundred professional papers that have won numerous top academic, professional, and business awards. He has provided advice, seminars, and presentations to senior leaders and managerial audiences throughout the world for more than forty years.

Among his more well-known books are the following: *Counting What Counts: Turning Corporate Accountability to Competitive*

Advantage; The Accountant's Guide to Legal Liability and Ethics; The Equity Funding Papers: The Anatomy of a Fraud; Making Sustainability Work: Best Practices in Managing and Measuring Corporate Social, Environmental, and Economic Impacts; and *Measuring Corporate Environmental Performance: Best Practices for Costing and Managing an Effective Environmental Strategy.*

KIRK O. HANSON recently stepped down as the John Courtney Murray, SJ, University Professor of Social Ethics and executive director of the Markkula Center for Applied Ethics at Santa Clara University. He has been a leading figure in the field of business ethics and corporate social responsibility for almost fifty years. He earlier taught business ethics and business-government relations at the Stanford Graduate School of Business for twenty-three years, where he was the faculty director of the Stanford Sloan executive master's program.

An active corporate and nonprofit consultant, Hanson has consulted with more than one hundred corporations on the management of business ethics and business scandals. He has spoken widely before corporate, academic, government, and civic audiences on ethical decision-making, how organizations create ethical cultures, and corporate leadership and governance. He has written a regular column on workplace ethics for the *San Jose Mercury News*; served as the founding chair of the Santa Clara County Political Ethics Commission; and was the founding Honorary Chair of the Center for International Business Ethics, China's first business ethics center. He was the founding president of the Business Enterprise Trust, a national awards program for exemplary behavior in business created by national leaders in business, the media, labor, government, and civil society. He has served on many nonprofit boards, including serving on the board of the Skoll Foundation for Social Entrepreneurship for the past twenty years. Hanson graduated from Stanford University and received his MBA from the Stanford Business School. He held research fellowships and appointments at the Yale Divinity School and the Harvard Business School. He has been awarded honorary doctorates from the University of Portland and Santa Clara University, and he was honored by the Aspen Institute Center for Business Education with a lifetime achievement award for contributions to business and society.

The authors previously collaborated on a four-volume series of edited books entitled *The Accountable Corporation*, whose volumes address corporate governance, business ethics, corporate social responsibility, and business-government relations.

Made in the USA
Coppell, TX
30 January 2023

11972785R00114